I0439067

THE CKD CAMPAIGN —

Leadership After Robert Mugabe:

THE ZIMBABWE INDUSTRIAL EVOLUTION

Retracing the Footpath of Kurumbi in the Galaxies (Gwara raKurumbi) under the Leadership of:

Chaitezvi Kanyuchi Dehwe

First Edition   Published in 2016

Available on:

Amazon.com: THE CKD CAMPAIGN — Leadership After Robert Mugabe:

THE ZIMBABWE INDUSTRIAL EVOLUTION

Youtube: CKD CAMPAIGN — Leadership After Robert Mugabe:

THE ZIMBABWE INDUSTRIAL EVOLUTION

Facebook: CKD CAMPAIGN — Leadership After Robert Mugabe:

THE ZIMBABWE INDUSTRIAL EVOLUTION

Twitter: @CKD CAMPAIGN — Leadership After Robert Mugabe:

THE ZIMBABWE INDUSTRIAL EVOLUTION

Table of Contents

Chapter		Page

	Introduction	5
1.	Manufacturing Economy	7
1.1	Zimbabwe Ultimate Development Milestone	7
2.	The Great Zimbabwe Sceptre	8
3.	Zimbabwe Traditions to Replace Roman/English/Dutch Law	9
4.	War Veterans, Collaborators, Detainees and Restrictees	10
5.	War Against Hunger	11
5.1	Mandatory 25% Small Grains Farming	11
5.2	Mandatory Household One (1) Year Grain Reserve	12
5.3	National Fruit Tree Roll-out	12
5.4	Irrigation Systems Development	12
6.	Restoration of African Identity	13
6.1	Hair Style at School and Work	13
6.2	Spiritual/Religious Tolerance at School	13
6.3	Optional Traditional Attire at School and Work	13
6.4	African Culture to be Taught in Zimbabwe Schools	13
6.5	African Language as Medium of Instruction in Schools	14
7.	Equal Access to Quality Education	14
8.	Housing For All by Year 5	17
9.	People Empowerment and Jobs – Economic Uhuru – The Crux of the Matter	17
9.1	Introduction	17
9.2	Reorientation of the Slave Mindset	18
9.3	Financing the Zimbabwe Industrial Evolution	18
9.4	The Illusion of Foreign or Offshore Investment	19
9.5	Projections of the Economy	20
9.6	The Market and the Greatness of Future Nations	20
9.7	Imperial 'Free' Trade Conventions and Protocols	21
9.8	Inverse Proportion of Economic Growth Among Nations	22
10.	Zimbabwe Industrial Evolution	22
10.1	Technology Accomplishment Targets / Milestones	25
10.2	Semi-conductor Manufacturing	26
10.3	Transport Industry	26
10.4	Oil and Gas – Resuscitation of the Feruka Oil Refinery	30
10.5	Toys and Games Industry	31
10.6	Space Science and Technology	32
10.7	Software Development	33
10.8	Information Communication Technology	34
10.9	Power Generation and Transmission Equipment	35
10.10	Lighting Systems	36
10.11	Instruments and Sensors	36
10.12	Industrial Tools and Accessories/Consumables	37
10.13	Farm Equipment	38
10.14	Mining and Earth Moving Equipment	39
10.15	Construction Equipment	40
10.16	Audio Visual Equipment	40
10.17	Broadcasting Equipment	41
10.18	Refrigeration and Air-Conditioning	41
10.19	People Moving Equipment	42

Table of Contents

Chapter   **Page**

10.20   Textile Technology and Processing   43
10.21   Military Hardware   44
10.22   Tertiary Institution Industrial Evolution Assignments   45
11.   Domestic Policy Issues   46
11.1   Political Policy Issues   46
11.1.1 Gun-less Society   46
11.1.2 The National Army   46
11.1.3 The Police Force   46
11.1.4 The Prison System (Mhosva Inoripwa / Ubadalo)   47
11.1.5 The Death Penalty   47
11.1.6 Anti-Poaching Laws   47
11.1.7 Guard Against Gender Abuse   48
11.1.8 Strategy Against Crime   48
11.1.9 Fight Against Corruption   49
11.1.10 National Registration and the Passport Office   49
11.1.11 National Health Policy   49
11.1.12 Use of Weed/Marijuana in Medicine and Spirituality   50
11.1.13 The Government   51
        (i)   Humility of the Leader   52
        (ii)   Presidential Residence – The State House   52
        (iii)   Remuneration of the President   52
        (iv)   Parliament and the Depoliticisation of Zimbabwe   52
        (v)   Appointment of Public Servant / Minister / Councillor   54
        (vi)   Public Sector Salaries and Transport   55
        (vii)   Traditional Leaders   55
        (viii) The Justice System (Mhosva Inoripwa / Ubadalo Concept)   55
        (ix)   Rape Offences   56
11.2   Socio-Economic Policy Issues   56
11.2.1 Unhu/Ubuntu   56
11.2.2 Abortion   58
11.2.3 Sodomy   58
11.2.4 Agriculture and Land Use   58
11.2.5 Clean Water for Citizens and Urban Rates   59
11.2.6 The Tax System   60
11.2.7 Early Nurturing of Entrepreneurs   60
11.2.8 Zimbabwe Marketing Corporation   60
12.   Foreign Policy Issues   60
12.1   Nuclear Trade Tariff   60
12.2   Environmental Pollution Tariff   61
12.3   Economic Approach to Racism   61
12.4   The African Union   61
12.5   United Nations Reform   62
        Conclusion   62
        Index   64

Introduction

Zimbabwe is facing unprecedented social and economic challenges and it is common knowledge to all the people of Zimbabwe that the expectations that people had of independent Zimbabwe have not come to fruition especially relating to socio-economic issues. Several methods including but not limited to religion, politics and economics have been tried on Zimbabwe to try to solve the challenges but none have yielded much, Zimbabwe has withheld her fruits from her people. Typical example is the case of diamond discovery in Chiadzwa, which seem to just have vanished or dried-up and a lot more resources hidden beneath the land of Zimbabwe will remain inaccessible as long as the citizens do not follow the requisite protocols. In view of these survival challenges, CKD is bringing in serious changes to Zimbabwe to which the land will respond by releasing fruits for the people to eat. If the citizens want to eat the fruits of Zimbabwe, CKD will be available to give the guidelines of elaborate procedures to be implemented correctly without making mistakes through trying some presidential wanna-be.

When the displayed colourful technologies that CKD is targeting Zimbabwe to produce within three (3) to ten (10) years are put into context, there are citizens with no self belief who are already questioning Zimbabwean capability by asking how a developing country will make such abrupt technological transition or evolution. Let the people of Zimbabwe hear it from an engineering point of view through a well exposed engineer in aero space, aviation including avionics or the cockpit, industrial process control, telecommunications, power systems and oil and gas. If any citizen was to visit a factory, will witness how easy it is to make a conveyor belt, electric motor among other equipment or even at home opening the vacuum cleaner will show how easy it is to make such devices, hapana zviripo makumbo enyoka when compared to the sophistication of the technologies of African fore bearers at Great Zimbabwe or Giza in Egypt achieved so many thousands of years back. It is so easy to make any device from air planes to aero space vehicles no wonder most business owners do not allow people into their manufacturing plants otherwise at the end of the visit, folks would be able to make their own airplane or turbo generator.

To demonstrate the ease of making technology equipment, the starting point in most medical equipment as an example of the CKD targeted technology is a sensor which in the measurement of body temperature is alcohol enclosed in a calibrated container, blood pressure measuring instrument is a balance between pressure due to blood circulation and manually pumped air of measurable value, blood centrifugal separator is simple circular motion, an x-ray machine is a generator/oscillator of electromagnetic radiation plus an imaging platform, an ultrasound scanner is another generator/oscillator of high sound waves plus a monitoring display and a microscope is a magnifying lens all of which are first or second year engineering student tasks easily achievable without supervision. The resuscitated Feruka Oil Refinery will use the same Laws of Thermodynamics used by Eng. Mbuya Muchigere in the preparation of sadza/ isitshwala for millennia when the north were still eating uncooked dogs (Hot Dogs) in Caucasus Mountain for reason of lack of the basic fire technology. Zimbabwean parents with engineering students in their homes can ask their children if they cannot achieve the targets set out in this CKD Zimbabwe Industrial Evolution. The people of Zimbabwe are too skilled to fail to achieve the CKD Industrial Evolution targets. What is missing in Zimbabwe or Africa in general is the engineering leadership at government level required to achieve these technological milestones for the reason that most African leaders are ancient Roman/English/Dutch law attorneys with very little technological skills to confront the key problem in Africa which is underdevelopment or lack of technology and whose psyche may prefer northern technologies to dominate in Africa in much the same way as Roman/English/Dutch law. All these targets set out by CKD are achievable bearing in mind that communal village farmers like Zimbabweans in countries like India and China are sending rockets into the aero space of which a rocket is just a weather proof container made of very high melting point alloys plus high precision guidance which if the right material is selected, welders at Gazaland in Highfields, Makokoba, or Green Market in Sakubva will equally achieve the same tasks performed by NASA contractors in America. It baffles the mind how a Roman/English/Dutch law professor cum politician gave away Zimbabwe Iron and Steel refinery plus associated national ore reserves for a song to some Indian villagers not better in skills than Zimbabwe, such agreements will be reviewed by the CKD government. The law professor preferred Indian brick layers to rehabilitate the iron and steel blast furnace, a task which can be performed by brick layers from Zaka, Dotito, Gokwe or Umguza among other places. Some of the colourful technologies depicted in this CKD Campaign document are manufactured in South Africa by semi-illiterate Boers then exported to the heavily PHDed Zimbabwe and the pertinent question to ask is, how do Zimbabweans justify their number one (1) ranking in Africa in literacy terms?

What is missing in Africa are leaders with the technological passion envisioned by CKD which the founders of the Great Zimbabwe were heading to had their development not been arrested by the effects of slave trade and imperialism when it can be observed that even linguistically Vanhu/Abantu had technology terms like Chitundumutsere-mutsere (space object) well before the advent of the Europeans onto the African peninsula. The Zimbabwe Industrial Evolution will be led by the Head of State as the technical kingpin or cog wheel with all necessary powers and oversight to ensure that local manufacturers are not disadvantaged by importation of junk equipment onto the market otherwise the Industrial Evolution will not bear any fruits if the whole country is not made to embrace it and achieve the set objectives. CKD will make day to day progress monitoring and follow-ups on the Zimbabwe Industrial Evolution target designs, prototypes and testing. CKD will review deep into design strengths like how adequate is the insulation and guidance control systems for Mlimo Space Vehicle 001 or Kurumbi CHT2, mindful of the causes of failure of American Challenger space vehicle. CKD will look closely into the efficiency of the hydro-electric generator and how good will be the dynamics of the motor brands Injiba and Ngwarati and their carbon dioxide emissions. CKD will check on the stability of the temperature control system for the Feruka Oil Refinery fractionating columns among other detailed checks to demonstrate the extent of detail that the Head of State will go in pursuit of quality and set milestone targets.

After the above simplification of Zimbabwe technological targets, If there still remains some among Zimbabweans who think *thina Abantu* cannot make these or better technological feats and compete with America, Europe or Asia, let those slaves stand up so that their ears will be perforated with eternal tags of servitude to other races. The use of African names for the Zimbabwe Industrial Evolution brands or products like Mlimo Space Vehicle 001, Kurumbi Space Vehicle CHT2, car brands Injiba and Ngwarati, Wezhira Steel Belt tyre, Mpfula Kahina 20 or Mvura Naya-Naya 20 for boom spray, Jakwara / Nhimbe 12 for combine harvester, Umlimi X01 for the tractor, Mvema for high speed or bullet trains, ZiNdege 102 (Zi-102), ZiNdege 103 (Zi-103) for two and three hundred passenger airplanes, Chigaduro GR50 for grader, Sahi for cutting instruments, Umoya for air compressors, Xirhami/chando for refrigeration compressors, Musoni for textile processing machines among other technologies is a strategy by CKD to create self belief among Zimbabweans that they can make and own their own brands. Confidence and sense of ownership will develop with time to the extent that people will celebrate or congratulate a brother or sister for buying a brand new 8 cylinder Injiba or Ngwarati motor vehicle and not BMW, Toyota, Peugeot or any other.

The CKD government will assist manufacturing enterprises in the Zimbabwe Industrial Evolution based on the categorised products such as Semi-conductors, Lighting Systems, Aviation Systems, Aero Space, Oil and Plastics, Toys and Games, Software Development, Telecommunication, Electrical Generation and Transmission, Construction Equipment, Audio Visual Equipment, People Moving Equipment, Earth Moving Equipment, Farm Equipment, Auto Mobile, Rail Transport, Instruments and Sensors, Medical Equipment, Refrigeration and Air-conditioning, Broadcasting Equipment, Industrial Tools, Textile Technology and Processing; to ensure that the formed enterprises will specialise in particular scope of equipment. The enterprises will start with core teams of experts with a team leader as opposed to the opulent and good for nothing chief executive officer or managing director but money draining titles, more employees will be added after the prototype stage. The CKD government will inject money required for initial enterprise phases of design, prototypes, testing and safety approvals before the enterprises start commercial production. After structuring the enterprises along the referenced specialization lines and giving financial support, Zimbabweans will do world wonders as done by their ancestors for the reason that to this day world historians, archaeologists and architects have no idea or clue how stones for the Great Zimbabwe were cut or hewed.

Developed nations today are as big as they are for the reason that the continent of plenty (Africa) is a sleeping giant and the CKD brief is to awaken the giant. There are more billionaires in America, Europe and Asia for the reason of more poor people in Africa and if the number of rich people increase in Africa, so will be a corresponding decrease of the rich people in America, Europe and Asia to the extent that their riches depend partly on African poverty which relates to African failure to add value to their natural resources and that is how tantalising it is. The ongoing Chinese advances in Africa is the new form of smart imperialism which is unacceptable and CKD understands that they are taking everything to China; diamond, gold, wood and above all dogs, they are even eating African dogs but the Europeans previously left Africans in possession of their dogs at least!! *Imbwa yangu Machena, Ah here-wohoye, yadyiwa nemaChina (Vadyi Vembwa / Bahlinja)*. Zimbabwe will be assured only of adapting to a dog meat diet with refrigerators full to the brim of dog meat from Chinese culture. How would the dog eaters from China help Africans migrate from poverty to milk and honey when the Chinese are not eating milk and honey but dogs?

The switch from Europe or the West to China by Zimbabwe is futile and valueless partnership that will not benefit Zimbabwe or Africa in general. Instead of encouraging African Industrialization to uplift the continent, developed nations consider that as economic suicide, instead they talk of win-win partnership with Africa where their corporations will come to Africa and build processing plants near the raw materials and not export raw materials to Europe, America or Asia. When processing plants are built near the raw materials by foreign corporations, Africans will get jobs while developed nations who own the foreign corporations, post super profits to their home countries, people can call it win-win partnership if they have a vacuum in place of a brain.

Chapter 1   Manufacturing Economy

The current buying and selling economy in Zimbabwe will come to an end as the Industrial Evolution comes to fruition. The Zimbabwean business philosophy will be required to evolve from buying and selling at street corners to working in factories with well organised and demarcated selling points/ markets.

Deliberate Loss Making Business

Growing cotton to export it raw while later importing clothing costing multiple times the value of the exported raw cotton is a deliberate and intentional loss making enterprise which is like economic suicide. Mining iron and associated alloys for export and then importing iron and alloy tools at hundred times the value of the raw metals is another example of intentional loss making enterprises which the CKD government will outlaw.

1.1   Zimbabwe Ultimate Development Milestone

Most development targets like the aircraft, the aero space vehicle and medical equipments among other technologies have up to ten (10) years to realise and when they mature, Zimbabwe will automatically migrate from a developing country to the developed world due to the fact that the population is made up of very educated people, who will be absorbed in the Industrial Evolution and put Zimbabwe on the same development stage or platform as countries like Holland and Luxembourg among other developed countries but India and China will remain behind as the number of uneducated and poor people will require more time and resources considering the fact that resource to population ratio in Africa is much higher than in India and China. To understand this statement one has to go to India and observe people's lives in the slums like Mumbai or the Mumbai train system which carries a world record of 14 passengers per square metre while in China, teacher-pupil ratio in schools can be 1 to 100 which is clear evidence of underdevelopment and compare these statistics to any place in Africa.

The development target set for Zimbabwe is easier to achieve for reason of massive investment that was done by Robert Mugabe from day one of Uhuru, people need to appreciate that. The CKD targets are huge and serious and will correspond to the greatness and fame of the Great Zimbabwe which was called great not only by its makers but even by its adversaries.

Chapter 2   The Great Zimbabwe Sceptre

It is without doubt that Robert Mugabe was/is the bona fide and first anointed leader of Zimbabwe from then until his retirement, which means that the Zimbabwe sceptre will be transferred from Robert Mugabe to another leader who may be within or without the existing polity. A look at the history of Zimbabwe during the liberation struggle and post independence era indicates that there was a sizeable list of credible candidates vying to lead Zimbabwe but Robert Mugabe has remained in control for reason of the scheme of the Great Zimbabwe and will remain so until another candidate appears and acceptable to take over by the same scheme and not only by popular democracy, no wonder Robert Mugabe has not picked a successor, for that is not his prerogative. Captaincy to the Great Zimbabwe is not by chance or luck but by the scheme of the Great Zimbabwe and so it is worthless sometimes to contest an election. Contesting as citizens may do any day, but as long as none of the contestants is acceptable to the Great Zimbabwe traditions to carry the sceptre, none will ascend the presidency up until the sceptre is given to the rightful candidate. If some power hungry candidate wants to impose self onto the sceptre, may die prematurely or his/her rule would be a disaster. If the bona fide holder of the sceptre fails to run the Great Zimbabwe in accordance with acceptable norms, his or her rule will be another disaster and if a wanna-be wants the sceptre, it will not land on the wanna-be.

During the reign of Robert Mugabe, CKD observed several citizens trying their luck and chance on the sceptre but even if a candidate has the support of today's most nuclear armed nation, if the sceptre of the Great Zimbabwe is not meant for them, they will not ascend. In that regard CKD observed candidates trying different methods to ascend but without this basic knowledge relating to the sceptre. The sceptre is not a monarchy and does not follow certain heirs but particular candidates with unique attributes not necessarily visible to popular democracy. The sceptre of the Great Zimbabwe is very special, because the present State of Zimbabwe was the capital city of vast Mwene Mutapa Empire which stretched across the breath of Africa and the president of Zimbabwe is like the virtual leader of the empire and that sceptre will not be bequeathed to some idiot and neither can money nor political clout play a role in determining to whom the sceptre will land. **Without giving detail, the protocol of the sceptre disallows CKD from challenging Robert Mugabe, the incumbent or bona fide holder of the sceptre and with that knowledge, CKD will not wrestle the sceptre from Robert Mugabe.**

The demeaning of the current bearer of the sceptre, Gushungo, by politicians of largely Roman/English/Dutch law background is clear manifestation of total ignorance and illiteracy of the Great Zimbabwe scheme of things and protocols, one wonders how such citizens want to lead the Great Zimbabwe with such meagre knowledge of it. The more Robert Mugabe is demeaned and insulted, the more is his life, health and power. How do folks aspire to be captain of the Great Zimbabwe when they have nil knowledge of it? Citizens can observe that there are fundamental differences in the political, spiritual, social, economic and technological approaches in addressing the Zimbabwean challenges between the CKD Campaign and the way Robert Mugabe has administered Zimbabwe from as far as 1980, but still that will not take away the honour, authority and respect of the first Captain of the Great Zimbabwe of this time nor provide an opportunity for CKD to demean or disrespect Gushungo.

The person who will assume the Great Zimbabwe sceptre will bring the prosperity exemplified in the precious minerals of the sceptre on cover page, not only to Zimbabwe but to the whole of the African peninsula and will be a key unifying leader in the quest for a United Africa. The prosperity to Zimbabwe and Africa will come from within including the financing of African renaissance; for Europe, America or Asia will not bring gold to Africa, their business with Africa has always been to export gold and precious minerals to their countries while exchanging the said gold with colourful bond paper that they call money. **The question of to whom the sceptre will land is now sealed and it is therefore prudent for the Zimbabwean polity to let the sceptre land where it intends to without hindrance.**

The terms and conditions of the sceptre are that if a bona fide holder of the sceptre fails to run the country in accordance with the acceptable norms of Zimbabwe, his/her term of office would be a disaster. If a wanna-be wants to hold the sceptre, it will not land on his/her hands and if for some reason a person forces self onto the sceptre, such a term of office would be another disaster. The upheavals or chaos in Zimbabwe polity can help people to understand the protocol of the sceptre. If the true bearer of the sceptre corrects the omissions of 1980, everything will fall into place considering the fact that **Zimbabwe 'inyika inoyera uye ine zviga zvayo / Ilizwe lingcweleyo'** which most citizens hardly understand but the colonial administration understood that and naming their office Mwene Mutapa Building was not by coincidence.

Chapter 3   Zimbabwe Traditions to Replace Roman/English/Dutch Law

Roman/English/Dutch law is not International Law as thought of by a few citizens but is the law of African subjugation, the law of imperialism or the law of the oppressor in which most facets of imperialism are imbedded. Nehanda, Kaguvi and Mlimo were tried and or executed by imperialism using Roman/English/Dutch law not because the three heroes had planted nuclear bombs in Rome, London or Amsterdam, but because they were defending the rights of their children and it is a shame for the victims of Roman/English/Dutch law to impose that brutal law around their necks. If there is going to be International Law, nations will convene on a same level platform to draw up the International Law agreeable and satisfactory to all nations without which the prevailing law will be Roman/English/Dutch. The current Roman/English/Dutch law inherent in the Zimbabwe Constitution is full of portions of culture, value system and history of the Romans, English and Dutch people including their gender preferences (sodomy) with no trace to Unhu/Ubuntu. There will be resistance against the repeal of Roman/English/ Dutch law in place in Zimbabwe today especially from the practitioners of that law from where they derive an income through the full administration of that law including commissions earned at every moment of property title transfer (title deeds) which CKD will annul. So these practitioners will wish Roman/English/Dutch law continue forever than institute a law based on African ethos, value system and traditions.

Prior to the colonial annexation of Zimbabwe, there was a functional state system with a leader, the people, judiciary, parliament (dare/ dale), land, economy, spirituality and culture. Upon the colonial annexation of Zimbabwe, the African system of governance and justice was replaced by the imperial Roman/English/Dutch governance system and on that fundamental basis, the people of Zimbabwe embarked on the Liberation Struggle which started off as the First Chimurenga War in the 1890s led by the legendary and greatest persons of this time Mbuya Nehanda, Sekuru Kaguvi, Mlimo, Mapondera, Mashayamombe, Mashonganyika among others and afterwards as Second Chimurenga War from 1960s to 1980 whose agenda was to regain African integrity on African land. So many innocent lives were lost while fighting the imperialists who had imposed their polity on Africa and so much consultation was done at African traditional and cultural level in order to attain victory in the war against the imperialists but what baffles the mind is that upon attainment of Independence in 1980, Zimbabwe remained subordinate to the Roman/English/Dutch polity and governance system by choice. What was the business of going to war with the European settlers if after defeating them Zimbabwe would still be administered by the polity or dominion of the settlers? Was it a foolish person's agenda for going to war? 'Don't you know me, I can fight anyone. *Ndinorwa semvumba ini, ndinombonzi aniko ini?*' Fighting for what? If the imperialists had pre-war knowledge of the fact that when Africans win the war, would still administer their African land with the polity of the losing imperial army, the imperialists would not have gone to war with Africans in the first place, but would have willingly handed over the reign to Vanhu/ Abantu with the full understanding that Roman/English/Dutch law would reign forever. What is the business of going to war over a piece of land if after victory the victor is not going to impose his or her polity or dominion over the piece of land that he/she fought for?

Wars over land are fought to impose victor's dominion over that land and not to impose the loser's dominion. In view of this logic, CKD will repeal the current Roman/English/Dutch Zimbabwe Constitution and institute a totally Zimbabwean constitution which shall be in accordance with the traditions, ethos and aspirations (Unhu/Ubuntu) of the founding mothers and fathers of Zimbabwe with a blend of applicable modernity. In short, the country Zimbabwe will be apprised to the Zimbabwean spiritual realm for the land to yield its fruits to the children of the Great Zimbabwe. Mistakes were done in 1980 in this regard but CKD will not blame Robert Mugabe who was brought up by the Roman Jesuits at Kutama for the reason that if Zimbabwe was to be handed on to the spiritual realm the wrong way, that was going to cause problems, **CKD who was brought up by a sanctified bull (*n'ombe yemudzimu / yinkomo yamadlozi*) will do the job**. The people of Zimbabwe have tried everything; orthodox church, evangelism, magicians and none of that has worked. If the mistakes of 1980 handover takeover are not corrected, the current generation and many to come will not eat the fruits of the land reminiscent of the cursed Hebrews of forty years and above who were destined to die in the desert from hunger, thirst, diseases and war among other curses, for the Great Zimbabwe will rather shed her fruits unripe than give to this generation.

The Zimbabwe justice system will be non-custodial but compensatory on the basis of the tradition of Mhosva Inoripwa / Ubadalo, the guilty party will not be kept in jail but will be allowed to work in order to compensate or pay restitution to the afflicted party.

Chapter 4   War Veterans, Collaborators, Detainees and Restrictees

Two great decisions of the past century in Zimbabwe were the resolution by Mlimo, Nehanda and Kaguvi to lead the struggle against imperialism in the 1890s and the resolve by boys and girls in the 1970s to forfeit their future and personal gains in order to pursue the objectives of the Liberation Struggle. CKD was too young to fight the Liberation Struggle but was old enough to understand the whizzing sound of a war red-hot bullet while herding cattle in the rural areas, the war veterans were angels who sacrificed their future to redeem the people of Zimbabwe from the brutality of imperialism and they deserve respect at national level. The war veterans, collaborators, detainees and restrictees were brilliant and selfless students who were top of the class doing sciences and arts at various schools across the breath of Zimbabwe. These brilliant and selfless students left class at ages 15, 16, 17, 18 or 19 where they were doing chemistry titrations, physics pendulums, frog dissections in the biology laboratory, integration and differentiation in mathematics or Shakespearean Literature but sacrificed and forfeited the degrees in engineering, medicine, law or a successful future, business or entrepreneurship and pursued the objectives of Uhuru. They left class without clothes, food and set off for gruelling hundreds of kilometre journeys to Zambia and Mozambique to fight to liberate Zimbabwe. Some died of diseases, some died of predator animal bites and some died of hunger, thirst and poverty. Some died of war and CKD remembers a song by war veteran Simon 'Dendera' Chopper Chimbetu, 'Ndarangarira Gamba' and in that song, the awesome spirit of a war veteran is given in graphic detail in that in one of the battles, a war veteran sustained a fatal chest wound and his comrades rushed to pick him up for treatment but the angel said no comrades, look I am at the point of death, don't worry about me but worry about the struggle and its objectives '*Ndarangarira musi watisiya gamba, mwana wenyu amai amire panguva yakaoma (moment of departure) handikanganwe kwete. Akashevedzera ndokushevedzera "Chionaika Comrade ini ndave neropa pachifuva, zvino topesana muupenyu, shinga Comrade, …. Katanurai zvikasha zvangu zvose muende mberi nehondo, fambai makashinga Comrade muchiti ZANU, ZANU"*. The ZANU that Simon 'Dendera' Chopper Chimbetu was referring to was the pre-Uhuru ZANU or ZANU before independence.

The picture of sacrifice by war veterans depicted in the song is too graphic, very patriotic and very generous. CKD is not an angel like that war veteran but a mortal who would have said '*Comrades throw your guns aside and carry me for medical treatment and we will resume the struggle later when I have recovered*' and would the liberation war have been won with that spirit? What would you have told your fellow comrades if you were fatally wounded in battle? Some of those comrades who died in the war were not given a descent burial but were eaten by the vultures, '*vakadyiwa nemakora*'. Upon attainment of Uhuru in 1980, the war veteran was uneducated because he/she left the chemistry, physics or biology class to fight to liberate Zimbabwe. With this background, most of the war veterans, collaborators, detainees and restrictees were demobilised at the end of the war with no reward in cash or kind only to find that those who had remained at school had become filthy rich and in high positions of government. The few war veterans that were incorporated into the Zimbabwe National Army in 1980 did not rise substantially in rank as a result of no education. Later some of the war veterans were given Z$50,000 gratuity in 1997 which at that time was worthy enough to buy a second hand car and today the war veterans, collaborators, detainees and restrictees are in sad sorry state after tremendous service to the Great Zimbabwe and with that in mind, the CKD government will restore the awe, honour and respect of maComrade / Magandanga / VanaMukoma by first resting the spirits of the departed liberation war fighters (Kuzorodza *mweya yevashakabvu iri kudzungaira mumasango*). Second, by thanking the war veterans, collaborators, detainees and restrictees (*Tozotenda vadzimba* (war veterans, dead and alive)), *'tisati tasuma nyama'* (Zimbabwe), for a job well done and give them national respect and recognition. Third, the CKD government will apprise the spiritual realm of Zimbabwe that Zimbabwe is back kuVanhu/Abantu (Zimbabwe *yauya, kwave kugadzirisa zvirango zvayo zvose zvadai kusunga michero kuti vana vadye*). Fourth, the CKD government will address seriously the welfare of the war veterans, collaborators, detainees and restrictees for sacrificing their personal life in pursuit of liberating Zimbabwe and fifth, the CKD government will assign war veterans, collaborators, detainees and restrictees to Defence, Security and Intelligence ministries, departments, and presidential advisers. Growing up as a little boy in war torn Zimbabwe, CKD was inspired by the war veterans, will want them to teach survival skills and the spirit of endurance in secondary schools. The CKD government will sponsor Hollywood proportion of motion picture — The Zimbabwe Liberation Struggle (Chimurenga War / Umvukela) from around the year 1890 as a way to celebrate, acknowledge and remember the role played by the collective people of Zimbabwe in the struggle for independence.

To demonstrate lack of adequate recognition of the role played by the war veterans, in Masvingo province as an example, there were mystical nom de guerres like Musa and Silas for liberation war fighters who were so popular even among the children that '*Musa or Silas would often visit Rhodesian Army barracks in the thicket of war, have breakfast with the soldiers and destroy the entire barrack upon departure*' but most of these gallant fighters did not get appropriate recognition after the war and lived a poverty stricken life and these veterans, the CKD government will cherish forever. Throwing teargas canisters today to peaceful gatherings of war veterans is a taboo or red line that the CKD government will not cross.

Pilgrimage to Chimoio/Nyadzonia/Tembwe on Foot by Born-frees

CKD will lead groups of born-frees on foot from Zimbabwe to Chimoio, Nyadzonia or Tembwe tracing the foot paths navigated by the freedom fighters which include crossing the rivers Zambezi, Kairezi, Save, Lundi and the wild life infested forests, to give young Zimbabweans the real feel of the sacrifice made by war veterans, collaborators, detainees and restrictees and experience the pain of the struggle. And when children learn of the Liberation War in class, they will have a clearer picture and can connect to it. Key in the pilgrimage will be hardship, reduced diet to come back home slimmer and more mature to understand the challenges in life far divorced from the contemporary spoiled children. The liberation war was started and coordinated by the priests (masvikiro/amadlozi – Nehanda, Kaguvi and Mlimo), assisted by traditional leaders, fought by the war veterans and supported by the war collaborators and the masses but after Uhuru, only a few privileged or connected people are eating the fruits of Uhuru largely through corruption, and CKD will seriously address such anomalies.

Chapter 5   War Against Hunger

5.1   Mandatory 25% Small Grains Farming

The CKD government will make it mandatory for every land holder in Zimbabwe (communal and commercial) including non-cereal farmers like tobacco, cotton or sugar cane, to farm drought resistant and more nutritive small grains (sorghum and millet) on twenty-five percent (25%) of their land. Most perceived droughts today may be normal seasons with low harvest as a result of trying to force northern climate crop varieties like maize corn and wheat on African savannah. Small grains resistance to dry spells is even knowledgeable to ordinary communal farmers yet there is no clear-cut policy from the minister of agriculture on small grains farming. Failure to comply with the 25% farming of small grains requirement will attract a penalty equivalent to average yield in tonnes per hectare of small grains times 25% of total farm area in hectares times average market price of one tonne of small grains. The cropping of small grains will be supervised by Chibero, Gwebi, Mlezi, Rio Tinto and Esigodini agricultural colleges to ensure that the set objectives are realised.

5.2   Mandatory Household One (1) Year Grain Reserve

Within one year in office, the CKD government will design a standard one year small grain reserve storage for communal and A1 farmers which by year three will be required to be full with surplus grain to feed the family or household for at least one (1) year. Reserve grain shall preferably be finger millet which is resistant to weevils and food alarm will be sounded if the reserve food store begins to be consumed before the next harvest. The household grain reserve will not be kept at the Grain Marketing Board as that will create unnecessary costly transport overheads. Farmers will also be trained on how to harvest hay in field drains for stockfeed capable of sustaining livestock for one (1) year.

5.3   National Fruit Tree Roll-out

The CKD government will through the Forestry Commission, in collaboration with Bulawayo Polytechnic and Mupfure Technical College, avail millions of free seedlings of both indigenous and exotic fruit trees to the people of Zimbabwe to reforest the whole country with fruit trees and not jacaranda (*anodyiwa here majacaranda avanaRhodes, haanhuwi bodo?*). Every household shall be required to plant one hundred (100) fruit trees (indigenous and exotic) within three years and on every anthill, there will be at least two indigenous fruit trees and recreate the Garden of Eden in the Great Zimbabwe. Citizens who fail to plant the prescribed fruit trees will prompt the CKD government to charge a land underutilization tariff or penalty for unnecessarily creating a hunger situation. Fruit trees will also be planted around each household plot of land in the communal areas, A1 or A2 farms including people living in urban areas for the reason that they will be required by law to coordinate with their communal homes in order to realise the one hundred (100) fruit trees per household planting target. The domestic trade in wild fruits which is in place today will have no buyers as every citizen will be fully stocked. It is much easier to survive in Africa than elsewhere in the world for reason of abundant natural resources; an unemployment rate of twenty-five percent (25%) may cause unrest in Europe or the West but a higher rate of unemployment in Africa may not be very noticeable for reason of natural endowments existing in the continent of plenty.

CKD remembers growing up in a well balanced ecosystem herding cattle in environs full of wild fruits and life was like a dream of picking fruits from all sorts of trees whose fruits were available all year round; *hubvu/tsubvu, shuma/shenje, nyii, hwakwa, mbambara, tsvoritsvoto, matamba, sosoti, rukato, mazambiringa, hute, maroro, zvidhororo, nhengeni, masawu, nzvirun'ombe, mauyu, matohwe, tsambatsi, mashuku/mazhanje, sika, nhunguru, hacha/chakata, mawonde, chechete, mapfura* among many fruits most of which are exclusive to Africa but are now severely depleted as a result of mismanagement of the environment when people started cutting down trees including fruit trees on large scale to clear land for agriculture or firewood without understanding that fruits are part of agriculture. Fruit trees especially indigenous fruits are manna from heaven which need no inputs nor work to harvest except to abstain from cutting the tree and in view of that mismanagement of the environment, the CKD government will make extensive reforestation of Zimbabwe to recreate the dreamland of the founding fathers and mothers.

5.4   Irrigation Systems Development

The CKD government will embark on extensive development of irrigation equipment and deployment to all regions in Zimbabwe as part of the Industrial Evolution in collaboration with Mutare Polytechnic, Masvingo Polytechnic and Africa University. The sum total effect of the above measures is that on any given year (low or normal rain season), the small grains will always nearly give the required yield while the fruits will be harvested and marketed all year round. Irrigation systems will provide the backup against droughts and Zimbabwe will not starve nor import food at any given time as people will be required to work and sustain themselves and any request for government food assistance will be accompanied by serious justification like an earthquake or volcano occurring in a particular household farm. Any food assistance where it is required will be provided by government agency and not donor agency.

Chapter 6   Restoration of African Identity

6.1   Hair Style at School and Work

School children will not be compelled to comb their hair so as to make it straight like Caucasian hair when going to school for the reason that Vanhu/Abantu are not Caucasian. African hair is kinky and curly and that is not criminal but who Vanhu/Abantu are, children may keep their hair lock like CKD as one form of African identity. Adults especially at work will be free to keep the lock of their hair (*mhotsi/ unwele olude*). African women will be re-oriented to buy more nutritive food for their lovely children than skin bleaching cosmetics or exotic hair make-ups. African people actually frown or twist their faces as a clear sign of discomfort or displeasure when combing their hair, like folks being forced to do something at gunpoint.

6.2   Spiritual/Religious Tolerance at School

School children will not be compelled to change their spirituality/religion in order to get a place at a church denominated school and will not be required to get baptised and bring the certificate thereof as a precondition for admission, as a measure to discourage religious extremism. Church denominated schools even go to the extremes of demanding baptism certificates for father, mother and ancestral church history of prospective students as precondition for admission and why would a little child be judged on the basis of religious schisms? Students will not be forced to attend church but will be given options to go for sports or study. Teachers of a particular religious incline will not be allowed to deviate from the syllabus and push their religious dogma on pupils/students. CKD who was raised in African Traditions was expelled from mission school after questioning the missionary requirement for students to kneel before some religious statues, the logic proffered by juvenile CKD was that Musikavanhu/ Umvelinqangi/Unkulunkulu taught by African elders would not be represented by motionless images which looked more like European folks moulded in concrete. The idea of religious tolerance required at mission schools is from the basis that mission schools were not totally built by missionaries alone but land was provided by Zimbabwe for free and over the years, all people from many religious/spiritual backgrounds have contributed to the construction of the mission schools in the form of building fund paid by parents and guardians for nearly a hundred years.

6.3   Optional Traditional Attire at School and Work

School children who wish to put on modest traditional attire when going to a school which has a prescribed school uniform, will not be compelled to put on school uniform but that their traditional attire of choice shall be acceptable. In the same context, workers who prefer their traditional attire at work will be allowed to exercise their right as long as such attire meet industrial safety requirements especially for workers who work with machinery or equipment.

6.4   African Culture to be Taught in Zimbabwe Schools

The CKD government will add two more subjects at primary school namely African Culture/Spirituality and Science and drop General Paper and one more subject in secondary school where African children will be taught the culture and value system of their founding mothers and fathers and how blessed it is to be African and to be bequeathed of the land of Africa and its huge resources. Key in African Culture will be Unhu/Ubuntu instruction, what distinguishes a human being from a dog because today the difference is now very narrow if it still exists at all, humanity is quickly morphing into dog culture but the dog remains more sincere than people especially when it wags its tail and dances in front an object, it will be sincere but not the human being. *Dog Culture includes barking at anyone or anything at every opportunity, lack of self respect, lack of shame, answering the call of nature in public, mating in public and with whosoever and eating anything that flies across the mouth including own vomit.* African children in the formative years will be required to memorise this dog culture (*umbwa/ unja*) and always reflect upon it in their transactions in life to see if they are deviating or converging with dog culture. The CKD kindergarten pupils will come home telling folks that what they were practising was not Unhu/Ubuntu but dog culture. The African Culture curriculum will include African music where Grades 1 & 2 will be required to be fluent in the *hosho/amahlwayi* or associated cultural instruments, Grades 3 & 4 will be required to be fluent in the drum (*ngoma/ingun'u*) and marimba while Grades 5, 6 & 7 will be required to be fluent in playing the *mbira/mbila* or associated cultural instruments for the reason that without African music there is no culture to talk about. O Level certificate will be required to have a compulsory pass in African Culture otherwise the certificate would be considered incomplete without African Culture and not English. Science subject will start in kindergarten school with the electric motor, demonstrating to kindergarten pupils that the motor is the source of movements in the toys which needs batteries to work and not porridge, that kind of language.

6.5   African Language as Medium of Instruction in Schools

As the Zimbabwe Industrial Evolution matures, African language will be made to adapt to technology terms to the extent that the medium of instruction in Zimbabwean schools will be African language noting that African people are learning multiple languages like English, French, Chinese, Russian among others in order to make themselves more marketable in European and Asian job markets. When the Zimbabwe or African Industrial Evolution matures, those nations without raw materials will naturally start chasing after African languages to make themselves more competitive on the African job market and languages such as Zulu, Shona, Ndebele, Kikuyu, Yoruba among other African dialects will be the foreign currency. The danger in trying to master all world languages in order to get more jobs is the loss in fluency in one's own language, culture and identity.

The Vanhu/Bantu Language or the African Language

In order to unify and foster closer integration of the various African tribes into one family as originally was, the CKD government will sponsor African Universities language departments to do research on the Vanhu/Bantu language in order to re-originate the Vanhu/Bantu language which was spoken by the founding MOTHERS and fathers before they separated and adapted to different habitats where they picked or dropped a syllable or so to result in the current Vanhu/Bantu dialects such as Kikuyu, Yoruba, Mandinga, Shona, Zulu, Xhosa, Ndebele, Shangani among other Vanhu/Bantu dialects. The Vanhu/Bantu language will become the official business language of Africa and medium of instruction in all schools and colleges/universities in Africa. The language of sodomy (English/French/Others) will die a natural death among Vanhu/Abantu.

Chapter 7   Equal Access to Quality Education

Quality education in Zimbabwe and the world over has been commercialised by the rich and middle class and only a few people can afford high performance private or mission schools which demand high school fees on admission to which the average child has no access. The rich and middle class have built schools and not factories to make money. School fees is now the tradeable merchandise and the CKD government will reverse that trend by providing a universal high quality education but low tuition fees affordable by the poorest with a target pass rate of 100% for both O & A Level within five years in office and parents will be relieved to know that whichever school they send their children, the quality of education will be the same due to the universal **One Class Model** by the CKD government. One hundred percent (100%) pass rate especially at O Level will mean that no student will drop-out at that level but that all the students will proceed to A Level and all schools will be upgraded to A Level with O and A Level classes having the same number of students for the reason that O Level is now like Standard 6 attained by the current great grand fathers and great grand mothers in the 1940s and 1950s. At the present moment it is every parent's nightmare to look for a good school for their children to have good quality education. Quality education is not universally available in all Zimbabwe schools but is limited to certain private or missionary schools often not accessible to many children/parents due to high cost of that quality education. When a good school is found, often it is far from home and the subsequent thirteen years would be gruelling for both students and parents while commuting to school and in the process, sacrificing a lot of time and resources to enable the child to access education at a particular good school. The CKD government will offer a quality and equal education to all children at all schools in Zimbabwe with top teachers, materials and study guide. There will not be any school drop-outs due to failure by parent/guardian to pay school fees.

The CKD Industrial Evolution will require artisans for industrial manpower but those artisans will be required to have at least A Level to fit perfectly in the Industrial Evolution and the Zimbabwe Education Curricula will be adjusted to dovetail to the Zimbabwe Industrial Evolution. Zimbabwe schools and colleges will be required to produce more science graduates than arts so as to have more factories than flea markets.

The CKD government will recruit the best twenty (20) teachers for each subject in secondary school to teach all subjects to all schools by large screen high quality picture and high quality sound cable television within five (5) years to create the Zimbabwean virtual class for Form 1 up to Form 6. The best Zimbabwean teachers will be interviewed and successful high performing teachers will be appointed to teach not one class but the whole country and the CKD government will give anything to this super team of teachers who will be known nationally as the super Chemistry, Physics, Shona or Ndebele instructors. All students in all Zimbabwean schools will be at the same level of the curriculum and receiving the best education from the best of the best teachers at the same level of school fees maybe twenty (20) dollars for secondary school as an example and not the current one thousand dollars ($1000) being charged by reputable schools with good teachers. Parents will not need to budget for school fees, but will withdraw the pet cash to pay for school fees from their pet cash cans. CKD remembers being expelled from school for non-payment of school fees, the other children will look at your misery as you pack your bags, poor soul. The remainder of the national teachers will be remedial or tutorial teachers at individual schools while the rest will be retrained and deployed into the CKD Industrial Evolution. A subject like Chemistry will teach all students the same lesson on Titration on the same day, or radioactivity will be done by all students in Physics the same day from Zimbabwe's super Mr. Physics and Biology students will dissect the frog the same day under the instruction of the best Biology teacher in the land, Ms Bio. CKD has come across students who sat for examination after only covering one third of the syllabus for reason of lack of qualified teachers among other resources.

When one student from Chilonga in Chiredzi telephones a friend in Mudzi, will remind her friend of the work done on a given date by a particular teacher (*Wakanganwa here dzidziso yatakapiwa naVaChidyamatovo musi wa2 Gumiguru?*). The individual schools will employ teachers for remedial work or tutorials based on the work covered by National Teachers administered through cable TV and a post lesson study timetable will be given to all students, boarding and non-boarding. All television channels accessible in the Zimbabwe territory will be required to add a study time alert at the corner of the screen to read; Red – Study Time or Green – Break or rest time in synchronization with the national study time table and preferably sounding a bell to indicate the start of study time in order to create a national consciousness on school or study among Zimbabwean students and during the national study time, the streets or public places will be expected to be clear of students and during vacation, students will rest as it was during the old days. It has come to CKD attention that most students do not cover as much ground on the syllabus as others or may never do any practicals at their various schools for a variety of reasons and inequality in the delivery of education, and the CKD government will end unequal access to education and afford all Zimbabwean children the same high quality education which is now limited to a select of Zimbabwean schools today and those money sharks that had invested in schools to harvest school fees from poor children, CKD advises them to convert those private school fees trapping machines into real factories to churn-out goods as envisioned by the CKD Zimbabwe Industrial Evolution.

To make teaching the One Class Model real, the national teacher will travel countrywide to make real life classroom instruction at different schools on rotational basis but that lesson would be broadcasted to the entire country for all other students to follow with normal interrupts by students or by inviting students to come to the board and solve problems with the other schools following suit but under the supervision of a local tutor. The national teacher may invite questions via teleconference or videoconference from other students in other parts of the country and the national teacher will move along the country; one week in Chiredzi at Chishamiso High School teaching Electromagnetic Waves in Physics, then move on to Mudzi at Kotwa High School to teach Radioactivity followed by another week in Matabeleland at Mzingwane High School teaching Medical Physics. Students all over the country will get to know each other through class participation that there is a hard to beat student called Hlomani at Mzingwane or Matigimu at Mwenezi. The crack team of national teachers will be considered key national assets and will be paid directly from the consolidated revenue.

School Assessment

The Zimbabwe school assessment will consist of course work and final examination with weighted marks of forty (40) % and sixty (60) % respectively. All the examination classes Grade 7, Form 2, Form 4 and Form 6 will have examinable course work. After studying about three (3) or four (4) chapters, the national teacher will set tests to be written on the same day at the same time by all schools and invigilated by neighbouring school instructors and marked by other instructors from within the same region. Surveys have shown that most students who fail examination are capable students who either panic on examination day or develop severe respiratory infection during examination which may seriously affect performance and therefore coursework assessment tests will provide fair assessment of student capability.

National Study Time Table

The CKD government will make a standard supervised study time table for both boarding and day school students (Session 1: 1715 - 1915 hrs, Session 2: 1945 – 2145 hrs) and these study times shall be supervised by father/mother or guardian with everyone working as a team to achieve 100% O & A Level pass rate as a CKD target within 5 years in office and the fathers will skip the bar when on study supervision duty as father, mother or guardian will be the boarding masters or mistresses for home boarding students. During the national study time, there will be no school pupil/ student loitering outside the study area nor will any student go to the market to sell merchandise, for school fees will be very affordable; municipal and national police will be authorized to deal with errant pupils/students found loitering. Study time will even start earlier than 1715 hrs as most pupils/students will enrol at the nearest school for all schools will have the same quality of education from the country's best of teachers. The One Class Model is necessary to reduce the cost of education by reducing the number of teachers who are a key component of education and who are better off working in industries than holding board duster. The CKD government will provide all households with school going children a basic solar lighting module to facilitate uninterrupted study for families who are not connected to the national electrical power supply grid. Primary school time table will be extended by one (1) hour and no pupils will take school work to their homes (homework).

Computer for Every Pupil/Student

The semiconductor technology and devices which include computers are getting cheaper day by day and more so when the Zimbabwe Industrial Evolution target of information communication technology matures. In view of the semiconductor maturity target, the CKD government will ensure that every school pupil/student will be equipped with a computer to make e-learning realizable. The central One Class Model learning system by cable television will be cheap to implement considering the fact that all equipment will be products of the Zimbabwe Industrial Evolution and the telecommunication backbone network will be able to provide fibre optic two way high quality video and sound from any Zimbabwean school to allow for more interaction between the national teacher and the other students in other schools or between students in different schools in the country.

Chapter 8   Housing For All by Year 5

There is a critical housing shortage in Zimbabwe for the wrong reasons – centralization of business and administration in the major cities of Harare, Bulawayo, Gweru, Mutare and Masvingo. CKD will decongest the major cities from new business investments by enabling small towns and growth points to grow industrially in order to spread the outreach of the national cake. The target groups that CKD wants to economically empower to be able to manufacture engines, electric motors and electronic chips among other technologies cannot afford inflated properties in Harare and other major cities and the majority of these new enterprises will do their businesses in small towns and growth points under close supervision of CKD who will be a full time rural resident and rural life with less noise, less pollution and more spacious will be more valuable like it is in real terms. Housing or industrial stands are very affordable in small towns and growth points which will be serviced by a high speed train system Mvema, run by Isitimela Corporation while internet will enable customers to view merchandise on websites without visiting the factory or through show rooms run by Zimbabwe Marketing Corporation. The current housing problem emanates from the illusion that Harare or Bulawayo are paradise, an illusion which pushes the prices of properties upwards.

There are fabulous places in Zimbabwe like Zvishavane, Plumtree, Mosi-oa-Tunya, Kariba, Karoi, Chiredzi, Nyanga, Chimanimani, Vhumba, Juliasdale, Lupane, Nyamandlovu, Nyamapanda among others where properties are affordable and these places have unpolluted environment and drinking water yet most people would die to pile themselves in a hell-hole called Harare while drinking water with floating human waste! People will be de-brainwashed from the belief that the value of people is measured by the cities or neighbourhoods that they live; good people in Makokoba or Dzivaresekwa can never be of less value or esteem to the thieves in Borrowdale or Mahlemhlophe who drive Porsche cars. These are social anomalies that have developed as a result of corruption and greed.

Chapter 9   People Empowerment and Jobs – Economic Uhuru - The Crux of the Matter

9.1   Introduction

Technologically there is a disconnection between the founding fathers and mothers who built the Great Zimbabwe thousands of years back and their descendants today. The world doubts if the Great Zimbabwe was built by African founding fathers and mothers for the reason that today their descendants are a far distant shadow of the founders and the CKD government will restore the link between the architects of the Great Zimbabwe and their lovely descendants. When the Great Zimbabwe was built by the founding fathers and mothers, the Caucasians who are the current technology leaders were living in Caucasus Mountain and eating uncooked dogs (hot dogs) as proof of lack of technology but today the same are so far ahead of the descendants of the architects of the Great Zimbabwe. If the tailing edge (north and west) are now sending space ships to Mars, the leading edge (Vanhu/Abantu) should be sending and landing space ships to outer galaxies external to this galaxy (Gwara raKurumbi) through such space vehicles as Kurumbi CHT2 to retrace the footpath of the legendary Kurumbi over and above Mlimo Space Vehicle 001 and the self belief used to build the Great Zimbabwe and Giza is key to the development of such technological feats and to that extent CKD has set milestone targets for Zimbabwe which are as great as the Great Zimbabwe.

The technological solutions required by Zimbabwe or Africa's needs today are made in the Far East, Europe and America by engineering graduates who are no different from Zimbabwean graduates with the same knowledge base but what distinguishes the other graduates is that their political leaders in the Far East, Europe and America provide them with the platform to solve all their user needs while in Africa the understanding is *'lets wait to see what the whiteman will do to our technology problems'*. Africa now urgently requires the leadership of hands-on engineering and design leaders with unrelenting self belief in order to re-establish the technology lead made by the founding fathers and mothers at Great Zimbabwe and Giza in Egypt when the north were still eating uncooked dogs (hot dogs) in Caucasus

Mountain due lack of the minimum fire technology.

As long as Africa or Zimbabwe do not evolve industrially, any economic upliftment of the people will just be piecemeal for the reason that the key problem in Africa, the land of gold, is technology and not finance.

Germany and Japan are today's successful technology leaders who emerged from World War 2 in 1945 as penniless villains but with CKD magnitude of determination and self belief, and on that basis any technology target that Zimbabwe and Africa set upon themselves to achieve is possible in order to confront Africa's chief problem — **lack of industrial technology which makes it difficult for Vanhu/ Abantu to benefit from the vast natural resources that the continent of plenty is endowed with.**

9.2   Reorientation of the Slave Mindset

The graphical illustrations of the Zimbabwe Industrial Evolution targets especially on the cover page depicting space technology, high speed trains and airplanes being manufactured by African people just like the Europeans or Americans are doing at Airbus and Boeing among other corporations will be bound to attract a lot of comments from the citizens of the form; '*CKD is an idealistic dreamer far divorced from the African reality*'. That mindset which says '*thina Abantu cannot attain that engineering feat*' is the mindset of an African slave to other races which CKD will without doubt eradicate among Vanhu/Abantu and it is an anti-development sickness or spirit of poverty which when eradicated will help reconnect the people to the founding architects of the Great Zimbabwe.

The number of jobs that will be created from the CKD Zimbabwe Industrial Evolution will exceed the available manpower to the extent that expatriates will be required to fill the job opportunities. The efforts led by Europe and America to eradicate poverty in Africa is just drama or a show or shedding crocodile tears because when they develop the under-developed countries then the market that was solely in the hands of Europe and America due to lack of development in Africa among other nations will be lost by the developed countries and therefore genuine desire for development must come from the under-developed nations as envisioned by the CKD campaign.

9.3   Financing the Zimbabwe Industrial Evolution

The CKD government will not approach any nation to finance the Industrial Evolution but will look from within as done by the founding fathers and mothers at Great Zimbabwe or Giza, who did not go to Rome, London or New York to beg for aid. Africa including Zimbabwe is the land of gold or finance and the gold of this land is geologically detailed by Moses in Genesis 2 vs 11-13 as:

[11] *The name of the first (river) is Pison: that is it which compasseth the whole land of Havilah, where there is gold;*
[12] *And the gold of that land is good: there is bdellium and the onyx stone.*
[13] *And the name of the second river is Gihon: the same is it that compasseth the whole land of Ethiopia.*

In view of the riches referenced above which were bequeathed to the people of Africa, the African people cannot then leave that gold and rich land to travel to the barren lands of snow and beg for gold when they are the proprietors of the land of gold, its absurd and stupid. It is the people of the land of snow who have to come to the land of gold to seek finance like they did through imperialism when they sought for gold, food and natural resources which is the finance and not the other way round. The CKD government will take the gold existing in the continent of plenty below the ground upon which Vanhu/ Abantu stand to finance any project as high and as huge as science can allow. What is the wisdom of mining gold in Africa the continent of plenty then take that gold to America to exchange it with some green bond paper and bring back that green bond paper with the illusion that Vanhu/Abantu now have finance? Or when Zimbabwe wants to do business with another sister country of gold like Zambia, what is the business of the green bond paper between the two nations? If the architects of the Great Zimbabwe thought dismally like that, then that edifice that continues to perplex civilizations to this day,

18

would not be there today. The founding fathers and mothers would have perhaps waited for Christopher Columbus to be born, set on a voyage to America, annex America and print the dollar, then the founding Zimbabwean fathers and mothers would start making contacts with America to get the green back to finance the construction of the Great Zimbabwe!! Africa with its mountains of gold will not be economically stable as long as people external to it benchmark or evaluate African resources but of course using the same benchmarks, the people of the land of snow will forever remain billionaires out of nothing while rich nations like the D.R. Congo with all its riches will be lucky to get junk status plus in credit rating when poverty stricken nations like Greece will walk away with half a trillion dollars of credit.

Zimbabwe is currently a $13.663 billion economy (2013) which is largely consumed by the import market and if through the Zimbabwe Industrial Evolution, market ownership is realised, the import market will cease to be in favour of major international corporations like Toyota, Mercedes Benz, Mitsubishi, Samsung, Sony, Apple and Microsoft among others and all that business will belong to Zimbabwe or Africa and those economic gains will trickle to each and every citizen and community.

Economic Savings from a Slim Government

The CKD government will consist of twelve (12) ministers (article 11.1.13) with no deputies and will be the slimmest government in the world and savings created from such a small government will finance the initial research, development and trial prototype production required to kick start the Zimbabwe Industrial Evolution.

9.4   The Illusion of Foreign or Offshore Investment

To this day Europe and the West have been doing business in Africa for about five hundred years in the form of bringing into the African peninsula a variety of vegetable seeds, cereals, sugar, guns and bullets as major trading merchandise and in turn they have exported human slave cargo, food and mega tonnes of precious minerals which is the finance which they used to develop their economies and nowhere in the history of human civilization have the north been known to have brought to Africa even one ounce of gold for Africa is so full of gold that when people walk to visit their friends' homes, they literally walk on gold ores, alluvial diamond or when they go to the river for fishing, they will find alluvial gold all over the river. CKD reminisces in childhood shooting birds with catapult loaded with shiny stones (rough diamond) and so foreign investment is the illusion of a foolish person searching for finance while standing on a mountain of gold. Africa, the very same golden ground upon which Vanhu/Abantu are standing is the finance and not some colourful bond paper from European Central Bank or US Federal Reserve Bank.

Most rich people of European origin were explorers who got their riches from the territories that they annexed or from the trade that they made while travelling but those that remained in the north were the poorest. The north is rich in snow and if the people of Africa are going to look for finance in the land of snow, they are sure to come home with packaged snow as the illusion of finance, the spirit of poverty hovering among Africans – 'shavi renhamo kana rakunanga unoswera uchiraura/redza hove muhari'. And so Vanhu/Abantu being the proprietors of the land of gold and the gold thereof, it can only be stupidity and absurdity that will send them to the land of snow (Europe/West) to look for finance. It is heart wrenching when the people of the land of gold die in the Mediterranean Sea while trying to smuggle themselves from the land of gold to the land of snow in search of wealth!

Even without talking about the abundant gold and precious minerals in Africa, the land itself which can support the most natural agriculture all year round is another form of finance or credit for the reason that as the global population grows and puts pressure on the planet especially for food, good land like African land shall be more valuable than silver and gold.

Economic Break-free

One of the objectives of imperialism was to take ownership of the market and resources in the colonies by destroying industrial and political capacity of the local people in the colonies and if the former colonies are to approach the imperialists to help them migrate from poverty to economic Uhuru, it will be like an ill patient approaching the same witch that caused the ailment for medicaments. The witch will without fail give another dose of infection. If a former colony requires to borrow money from IMF or World Bank, the same banks will say that the former colony has junk status credit rating and therefore basing on the grand scheme of imperialism, the witch will not give remedy to its ailing victim but more infection and the only way that the ill patient (former colony) can heal is to break free from the imperial economic system and benchmarking with separate credit rating agencies or stop consulting the witch.

And therefore any African politician who will campaign with promises of a prosperous future to the people of Africa based on European/ Western finance for general social, economic and substantial industrial upliftment of the people of Africa, that politician would be illiterate in leadership terms.

9.5   Projections of the Economy

Zimbabwe with a GDP of about $13.663 billion (2013), exports raw materials of value of about $3.507 billion consisting of mainly unprocessed nickel ores, platinum ores, ingot gold which is not value added, rough diamonds and cured tobacco all of which when value added will produce products with market prices which are five to ten times or more the value of raw ores which basically means that Zimbabwe should be earning at least $35 billion dollars in export business if the CKD Industrial Evolution was in place at this day. If $35 billion export business is added cumulatively in retrospect of 2009 (seven) years, the accumulated export earnings would be $245 billion earned by Zimbabwe since 2009.

Lost Business Due to Imports

Zimbabwe imports goods and services worth about $7.7 billion (2014) a year largely consisting of everything ranging from oil, food, clothing, electricity, fertilizer, motor vehicles, medicaments among other needs with a retrospective cumulative total from 2009 of $54 billion.

Projected GDP at Zimbabwe Industrial Evolution

If the above gains of Industrial Evolution are factored into the Zimbabwean economy, retrospect cumulative gains from import and export business opportunities would have earned Zimbabwe a total of $299 billion from 2009 and the current GDP would be a minimum of $43 billion and not the $13.663 billion of poverty. On that basis, Zimbabwe has all it takes to lip-frog from a developing nation to a developed country and join other members as indicated in the Zimbabwe Ultimate Development Milestone article 1.2 and CKD has clear guidelines on how to achieve that feat.

9.6   The Market and the Greatness of Future Nations

The greatness of future nations will be measured not by the number or size of their nuclear warheads but by the size of their market. The size of the market shall depend upon the amount of natural resources that a nation is endowed with for the reason that all nations will evolve industrially to be able to add value to their natural resources such that those nations with more natural resources will have a bigger market. There will be no nation that will import third party raw materials to create value addition jobs and wealth for its people and there will be gnashing of teeth (*kuchava nokugeda-geda kwameno / amazinyo azagegeza*) among those nations especially from the north that are largely endowed with snow yet have trillion dollar economies derived from third party raw materials value addition. Typical example is Greece which hardly has anything of economic value except a shore line for tourism and some small scale fishing yet Greece can borrow about $400 billion when the D.R. Congo ($60 billion economy - 2014) which is bigger in natural resources than Europe's super ten nations comprising United Kingdom, Germany, France, Spain, Holland, Belgium, Italy, Portugal, Luxembourg and Austria which have a combined economy of $14 trillion – 2014, would be required to produce countless securities in order to borrow just one (1) billion dollars, the zenith of economic injustice and partiality.

What is happening to Greece and other weaklings in the European Union is precursor to the gnashing of teeth referenced herein which will come when the sources of raw materials for European, American and Far Eastern Industries evolve industrially and begin to add value to their natural resources as envisioned by the CKD Campaign.

The CKD government will take ownership of the Zimbabwean/African market, guard it and consider it as a survival tool without which a people or a nation will extinct. The market is like land or a spouse which is a personal belonging and which cannot be doled-out to other nations, like marrying a spouse and then sending her to India or China for honeymoon with some Chinese or Indian dude over there or issuing a title deed to a third party over your land, its absurd and unreasonable generosity. The ownership of the African market will be coordinated at African Union level for quota system production of goods out of raw materials in that geographical domain. The French farmers are at war with their government against the importation of foods to France at their expense and that is where every nation is heading to.

At this dawn of the Zimbabwe or African Industrial Evolution, the current market leaders like America, Europe and Far East will shrink to their natural sizes and the *gnashing of teeth* aspect of that shrinkage is that their populations have lived large for centuries on third party resources or are not used to living their natural sizes like spoiled folks and in the history of nature, there are rarely stories about transforming spoiled people or animals to live a normal life, often species or civilizations extinct than try to make extreme adaptations. Will today's developed nations be able to adapt and live on one dollar a day that they are so fond of talking about in relation to hard life in developing nations, when their market and dominance shrink to natural size?

9.7   Imperial 'Free' Trade Conventions and Protocols

For two hundred years of imperial subjugation, Africa could not freely send her children to school or do scientific industrial research and for that reason industrial development was marginal no wonder today fifty years after independence, industrial capacity has not matured. In this context, the industrialized imperial nations want Africa and the developing world to adhere to free trade rules when industrialization is not globally at the same competing level. Free trade protocols and conventions forced on developing nations are simply laws to protect the industrial lead or gains of imperialism. It is not free and fair trade for industrialized nations to compete on free market basis with developing countries. How do countries which cannot make a needle compete freely with those that are sending space vehicles to outer space? How do developing nations agree to free trade conventions with industrialized nations when they cannot make even a needle? The market needs to be closed from cheap GMO food imports, cheap quality cars or cheap quality clothing or any other cheap quality merchandise from industrialized nations to encourage developing nations to grow industrially to be self-sufficient. When Zimbabwe or Africa closes its market, chants of 'free trade' will be made by developed nations to force Zimbabwe or Africa to abide by the imperial trade conventions where they will sound alarm bells that 'free trade' provisions of Roman/English/Dutch law have been violated. Zimbabwe or Africa are not Romans/English/Dutch to be required to be bound by such laws but are Vanhu/Abantu. Vanhu/Abantu do not owe anyone or any nation anything and if there is anyone among Vanhu/Abantu who feels indebted to any nation or law, sorry to that slave, *tine urombo nenhapwa iyoyo*.

Most growth projections made for the developing and developed world assume that the developing countries will forever be developing and continue to pump raw materials to the developed world and those developed world markets do not envisage a scenario that the developing countries will soon evolve industrially as envisioned by CKD.

21

9.8   Inverse Proportion of Economic Growth Among Nations

The global resources are finite and cannot be amplified for all nations to grow at the same time. Europe, Far East and America are great economies today for the reason of subjugating other nations through imperialism. The developing world has no industrial capacity and so they export raw materials which the developed world process to grow their economies at the expense of the sources of the raw materials and there is therefore an inverse relationship of growth between developed and developing nations. If developing nations like Zimbabwe evolve industrially to be able to add value to their natural resources, it means a loss of raw materials, value addition jobs and market for developed countries, and to the developing world it means more jobs for citizens, bigger market acquisition and real economic growth and so when millennium development goals or general economic upliftment of life is mentioned by developed nations to developing countries, its just pretence because Europe, Far East and America know pretty well what it means to their market, value addition jobs and economic growth of their countries if the developing countries evolve industrially, it means Armageddon, no wonder they keep on clinging to nuclear arms of war, it may be necessary to threaten force to third party resources or nations when push comes to shove. Europe, Far East and America have a history of barbarity and morally it is not an impossibility to their conscience to resort to that line of action and that is why it is critical to disarm nuclear nations using economics as indicated in article 12.1 Nuclear Trade Tariff in this campaign document.

Often Europe, Far East and America do not talk of African Industrialization for that will be suicide on their part but what they are fond of expressing is 'win-win' partnerships between them and Africa where they will continue to process African resources either in the Far East, America, Europe or coming to Africa as large multi-national corporations processing African raw materials and making huge profits to repatriate home while Africans get slave salaries where Africans will continue to lose the full value of their natural resources and nowhere near win-win situation. Listen to them at their economic meetings especially at places like Davos Economic Forum where they discuss their profits, losses and future growths, they will not make the mistake of helping industrialise Africa for that will be the end of American and European dominance and this is the challenge that CKD is taking head-on for the betterment of the impoverished African child for the reason that when CKD sees multinational corporations mining and exporting millions of tonnes of platinum, gold and diamond in the neighbourhood of starving African children, the heart bleeds.

For the record, the foundation of America was built on the back of unpaid African slave labour and so when America was growing through slave trade, Africa lost human power to advance its growth and the inverse relation of growth among nations continues to this day, while they dole-out plastic smiles accompanied by several hand-shakes.

Chapter 10   Zimbabwe Industrial Evolution

[**Note** – CKD is an Electronics and Electrical engineer with more than twenty-five years of hands-on experience in aviation, aerospace, telecommunication, computing, electro-mechanics, oil and gas, industrial control and automation]

The CKD government will consider the Zimbabwean or African market as the most valuable asset or possession which will be unimaginable to dole-out to Europe, Far East, China, India, Brazil or America. By exporting raw materials and importing finished goods which are fabricated from the same exported raw materials, Zimbabwe and other developing nations are giving away or exporting jobs and empowerment opportunities of their people and on that basis, the industrial value addition targets on page 25 shall be made and fulfilled by the CKD government without fail with signature footprints of the architects of the Great Zimbabwe but now being produced by their descendants.

Zimbabwe Appetite for Success

The people of Zimbabwe have tremendous appetite for greatness and the colourful images of devices illustrated in this campaign document that will be made by the people of Zimbabwe through the Industrial Evolution will motivate them to aim even higher. 'Tisu anhu acho ari kuita zviro izvi'.

Industrial Patents to Develop Universities

The CKD government will sponsor research that will design products in collaboration with universities and technical colleges in Zimbabwe and the patents thereof will be owned by the government and tertiary institutions to help small enterprises off-load the burden of research and universities will benefit from the patents as a way to earn money for university development. Patent ownership by Zimbabwean universities will make the universities more strategic and autonomous with very serious international ratings and enterprises that will manufacture goods based on a particular university patent will be levied a small fee for the patent owner. Working in collaboration with manufacturers will make Zimbabwean universities as competent and competitive as any other top ranked international universities like Massachusetts Institute of Technology, Harvard, Cambridge among others and students from all corners of the world will come to learn in Zimbabwe universities. Zimbabwe engineering undergraduates will be required to make an improvement to any Zimbabwe Industrial Evolution technology as a continuous improvement strategy to keep Zimbabwe products always top of the range, without which the students will not graduate. Zimbabwe universities will be equipped with skilled instructors, researchers, new departments and equipment to enable them to handle the demands of the Zimbabwe Industrial Evolution. As examples, National University of Science and Technology will be equipped with the Aero Space Engineering Department with full facilities to research on the aerospace plus an aerospace testing facility with a Control and Command Centre at Thorn Hill Air Base in Gweru and University of Zimbabwe will be equipped with the Department of Aviation and Aircraft Engineering with full facilities to research on the airplane plus a testing facility at any of Zimbabwe international airports. Technical colleges in Zimbabwe will be upgraded to universities to co-exist with the existing polytechnics to become Universities of Harare, Gweru, Kwekwe, Bulawayo, Masvingo, Mutare, Kubatana, Msasa, Mining, Kushinga Phikelela, Mupfure, Westgate, Chibero, Gwebi, Rio Tinto, Mlezi, Esigodini, Forestry, Harare Institute of Technology and will be equipped with all the necessary tools, infrastructures and resources to be able to achieve the CKD set objectives.

The Timing of the Zimbabwe Industrial Evolution

In 1980 at Uhuru, the Industrial Evolution was not technically possible for the reason of skills shortage especially among the indigenous people but in the year 2000, twenty years after independence it was technically feasible to start the Industrial Evolution but that was not done and most engineering experts have migrated to developed nations where they are manufacturing most of the devices proposed in this document. What is visible today on the Zimbabwean job market are a lot of university graduates in political and social sciences to the extent that today there are more indigenous Non-Governmental Organizations (NGOs) than indigenous industrial manufacturing companies. There are NGOs of the form Centre for Democratic Studies, Centre for Peace Dynamics, Coalition of Political Scientists among others and none of these organizations make any industrial merchandise but what they do is make a lot of preposterous political speculations on Zimbabwe which do not help the nation at all. In order to achieve the targets set out in this Zimbabwe Industrial Evolution, CKD will be on the frontline, every step of the way; on the design desk, on the test bench, in the test laboratory and in the field and will not delegate this key assignment.

Manufacturing Internship

The CKD government will avail the services of manufacturing specialists in collaboration with National University of Science and Technology Department of Industrial and Manufacturing Engineering to help most new manufacturing companies to fabricate the goods from patent through various processes to the final products that Zimbabwe needs like demonstrating what equipment and material are required to make a drilling machine, a lathe machine, a screw driver, a drive belt, a toy, an electric motor or how to load *'Ehu-uwe Nyarara Mwana / Thula Mntwanami'* onto a toy among many goods required for the Zimbabwe Industrial Evolution. The Great Zimbabwe has worked in iron and associated alloys for thousands of years prior to the advent of the Europeans through *mvuto nemhizha / Isisebenzi sidalansimbi* (metal engineering) and will not fail to make steel or alloy tools now. Value addition will be a key theme of the Zimbabwe Industrial Evolution and as an example, no raw granite stone will leave Mutoko, but stone cutting factories will be set up in Mutoko to export finished and polished stones for floors, walls, roofs, bathrooms and kitchen tiles among other uses.

10.1 Technology Accomplishment Targets/ Milestone Table

S. No.	Technology Accomplishment Description	Target Date
10.2	Semi-conductor Manufacturing	3 years
10.3	Small Vehicles 2.5cc, Motor Bikes and Bicycles	3 years
	Small to Medium Trucks 2-5 Tonnes	5 years
	Large Trucks, Buses, Earth Movers and Excavators	7 years
	High Speed Trains (Mvema)	7 years
	Passenger Airplanes 200 and 300 seaters	10 years
	Passenger Airplane Engines	10-15 years
	Aviation Support Systems	4 years
10.4	Oil and Gas – Resuscitation of Feruka Oil Refinery	3 years
10.5	Toys and Games Industry	Day1
10.6	Space Science and Technology	5 years
10.7	Software – Operating Systems, search engines, internet navigators, Anti-viral, Social Networks, Apps, PLC	3 years
	Applications Systems and Data Bases	4 years
10.8	Information Communication Technology passive devices	1 year
	Mobiles Phones and Computer Hardware	4 years
	Routers, Switches, Transmitters, Receivers and Multiplexers	7 years
10.9	Power Generation and Transmission Equipment	3 years
10.10	Lighting Systems	3 years
10.11	Industrial Instruments and Sensors	5 years
	Weather Sensing and Reporting	3 years
	Medical Equipment	5 years
10.12	Industrial Tools and Accessories	3 years
10.13	Farm Equipment	5 years
10.14	Mining and Earth Moving Equipment	5 years
10.15	Construction Equipment	5 years
10.16	Audio Visual Equipment and Cameras	4 years
10.17	Broadcasting Passive Equipment	1 year
	Broadcasting Active Equipment	5 years
10.18	Refrigeration and Air-Conditioning	3 years
10.19	People Moving Equipment	3 years
10.20	Textile Technology and Processing	3 years
10.21	Military Hardware	Nil

10.2   Semi-conductor Manufacturing

The Zimbabwe Industrial Evolution envisioned by CKD will depend on Zimbabwe's advancement in semi-conductor electronic devices for the reason that every technology today has an imbedded intelligent electronic device. Medical equipment, industrial tools, toys, motor vehicles, aeroplanes, aerospace vehicles among other technologies are run and controlled by an intelligent chip or computer system and to make this technology evolution successful, CKD will not delegate this key assignment but will assume that responsibility which means that the semi-conductor manufacturing vehicle will be under the direct auspices of CKD to be able to churn-out integrated circuits, processors, controllers, components and devices required within three years in government in collaboration with National University of Science and Technology Department of Electronics.

Semi-conductor Manufacturing in Collaboration with National University of Science and Technology

10.3   Transport Industry

The current assembling of Asian and European car brands by some of Zimbabwean or African car assemblies or the assembling of television sets by Samsung or others in Africa is not the Industrial Evolution envisioned in this document. A Mazda vehicle manufactured in Japan and shipped to Zimbabwe in the form of kits is a totally Japanese car benefiting largely the Japanese economy. The Industrial Evolution referenced herein starts from raw material such as iron ore through all the processing stages until the finished product like a car is realized which creates a lot of jobs and empowerment opportunities along the chain whereas the assembling of European or Asian cars in Zimbabwe only creates a sales person out of the possible myriad of jobs and empowerment opportunities. For the record, in the year 2014, Zimbabwean transport consumers imported motor vehicles worth $469 million and this is the market that Injiba and Ngwarati will totally own 100% to empower Vanhu/Abantu and not America, Europe or Asia.

(i)   Small Vehicles 2.5cc, Motor Bikes and Bicycles

It is unimaginable that the descendants of the architects of Giza and the Great Zimbabwe cannot make a bicycle four thousand years later. **The key question is; do the descendants of the architects of the Great Zimbabwe need to import even bicycles from other nations?**

In view of the above key question, within three years of the CKD government, small vehicles of up to 2.5cc engine capacity like Injiba and Ngwarati among others will be designed and manufactured in Zimbabwe by indigenous enterprises with other components that make up a motor vehicle like tyres, batteries, alternators, starters, auto-electrics and controls, bearings, exhausts, radiators and coolants being made by specialist enterprises within Zimbabwe. Car manufacturers will work in collaboration with auto mobile specialists recruited by the government, Midlands State University, Gweru Polytechnic and Kwekwe Polytechnic as the centre for auto mobile research and development. The first year will be for design work, the second year will be for prototype development and testing and the third year will be full production of Injiba and Ngwarati for the market and the Great Zimbabwe children will lift the flag thereof at international vehicle exhibitions and *ubaba lomama ekhaya bayathi bonani abantwana bethu khonapo.*

Small Vehicles, Motor Bikes and Bicycles Manufacturing in Collaboration with Gweru Polytechnic, Kwekwe Polytechnic and Midlands State University

The importation of vehicles and assembling of foreign vehicle brands will be phased out as follows to create the necessary local demand needed by Injiba and Ngwarati among other local brands: In the first year of the CKD government, motor vehicle consumers in Zimbabwe will be allowed to import 66% of their motor vehicle needs and in the second year will import only 33% of their motor vehicle needs and in the third year, the Zimbabwe local car brands would be rolled out from Zimbabwean factories and therefore importation of any other brand of small cars like Toyota, GMC, Chevrolet, Nissan, Mazda, Mitsubishi, Mercedes, Renault, Citroen, KIA, Hyundai among others will cease so as to create serious empowerment opportunities to the people of Zimbabwe and own the market. In that regard, a brand new Injiba or Ngwarati motor vehicle will come ideally not with Bridgestone or Yokohama tyres, but with Wezhira Steel Belt tyre to make them wholly Zimbabwean cars to benefit the Zimbabwean economy as an example of total market ownership.

(ii) Small to Medium Trucks 2-5 Tonnes

Within five years of the CKD government, Zimbabwe will be churning out its own small to medium trucks 2-5 tonnes along the same lines as small vehicles with exports to the African market through the African Union trade laws to empower the previously disempowered people of Africa. In the first year of the CKD government, small to medium truck consumers in Zimbabwe will be allowed to import 75% of their motor vehicle needs, in the second year will import 50% of their motor vehicle needs, in the third year will import 25% of their motor vehicle needs and in the fourth year there will be no imports of vehicles in this category in order to create the local demand required to sustain the local manufacturers. The Zimbabwe motor vehicle brands Injiba and Ngwarati will come in all types and models in order to cater for all transport needs — sedans, SUVs, pick-ups, 2-5 tonne trucks, lorries and heavy long distance trucks.

(iii)   Large Trucks, Buses, Earth Movers and Excavators

Within seven years of the CKD government, Zimbabwean enterprises will be manufacturing Zimbabwean brands of large trucks, buses, earth movers, and excavators along the same lines as small vehicles and trucks above with export market to the African Union in collaboration with Bindura University of Science Education, Msasa Technical College, Kubatana Technical College and Westgate Technical College. In the first year of the CKD government, consumers of large trucks, buses, earth movers and excavators will be allowed to import 84% of their large truck needs, 67% imports in the second year, 51% imports in the third year, 34% imports in the fourth year, 17% imports in the fifth year and no truck import in the sixth year in order to create the demand required to sustain Zimbabwean brands of large truck manufacturers.

(iv)   High Speed Trains

Within seven years of the CKD government, Zimbabwe through Isitimela Corporation in collaboration with Lupane State University and Bulawayo Polytechnic, will be designing and manufacturing its own High Speed Trains branded Mvema which will be as equally competitive as Alstom, Bombardier, Siemens, Kawasaki among other international brands for the local market and export to the African Union like the Europeans are doing in the European Union.

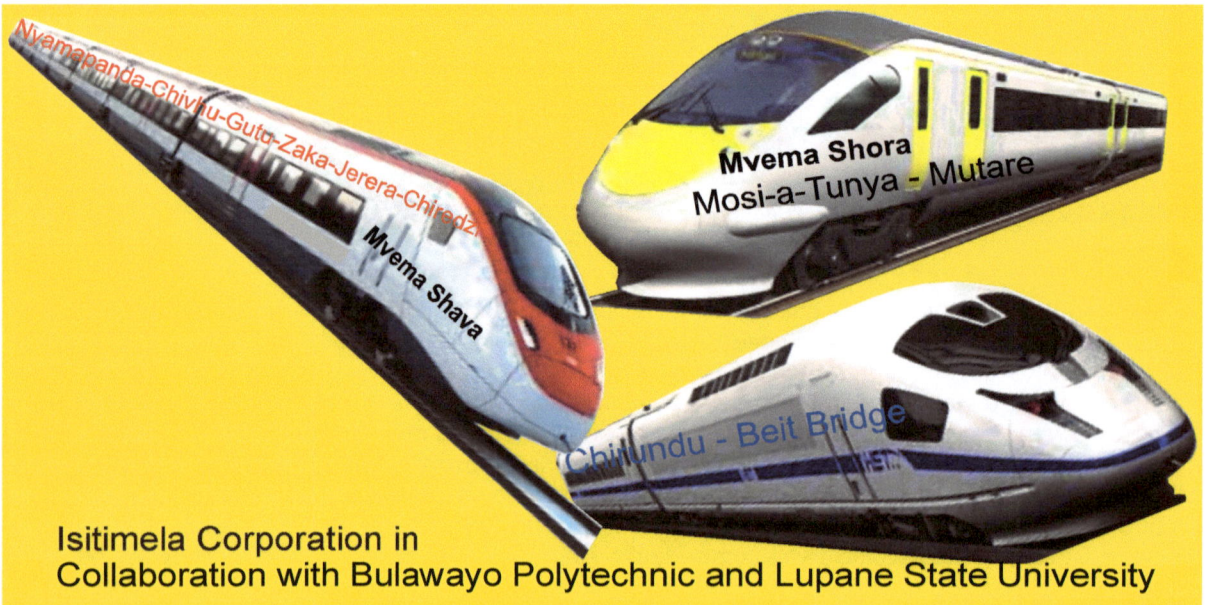

(v)   Passenger Airplanes

Within ten years of the CKD government, Zimbabwe through ZiNdege Corporation in collaboration with University of Zimbabwe School of Aviation and Aircraft Engineering, Harare Polytechnic and Mupfure Technical College, will be manufacturing 200 passenger planes ZiNdege 102 (Zi102) and 300 passenger planes ZiNdege 103 (Zi103) which will be completely different and distinct airplanes with different aerodynamics whose engineering basis will be greater than a combination of Isaac Newton and Daniel Bernoulli mechanics, different aesthetics and extra fall safe features and passenger handling configurations to be given to manufacturers by CKD but engine manufacturing will continue to be outsourced from the current international manufacturers including but not limited to CFM International, General Electric, Rolls Royce, Pratt & Whitney and International Aero Engines until the maturity of local engines. Passenger airplane consumers will be allowed only to lease airplanes for the first ten years of the CKD government in order to create the necessary demand required to sustain ZiNdege. ZiNdege Corporation will compete with Airbus, Boeing, Lockheed Martin, Embraer, Bombardier and Cessna among other manufacturers to give the people of Zimbabwe the competitive edge of the founders of the Great Zimbabwe but the African Union market will be skewed in favour of African manufacturers. Air and high speed rail modes of transport will dominate future transport and thina Abantu need to have a share of that business by all means.

ZiNdege Corporation in Collaboration with Harare Polytechnic, Mupfure Technical College and UZ School of Aviation and Aircraft Engineering

(vi)   Aviation Support Systems

Within four years of the CKD government, Aviation Support Systems such as 400 Hz Aircraft Power, Passenger Boarding Bridges, Aircraft Docking Guidance Systems and Baggage Handling Systems among other aviation support systems will be produced by indigenous Zimbabwean enterprises for the Zimbabwean and African Union market through ZiNdege Corporation in collaboration with University of Zimbabwe School of Aviation and Aircraft Engineering, Harare Polytechnic and Mupfure Technical College to compete with Thyssen, Safegate, FMT and Honeywell among other manufacturers.

ZiNdege Corporation in Collaboration with Harare Polytechnic, Mupfure Technical College and UZ School of Aviation and Aircraft Engineering

As an example of the simplicity of technology, 400 Hz Aircraft Power is power designed for use in aircrafts to reduce the weight of airborne equipment, is an elementary rectifier AC to DC converter followed by DC to AC inverter plus an oscillator which can be designed and fabricated by high school physics class but in Africa that elementary circuit is shipped all the way from Texas, USA or Stockholm, Sweden while Zimbabwean or African engineers are selling vegetables at Sakubva, Makokoba, Mucheke or Mbare vegetable markets, what was the business of spending so much money training engineers when they eventually specialise in vegetable vending?

10.4   Oil and Gas – Resuscitation of the Feruka Oil Refinery

Prior to Uhuru in 1980, Zimbabwe had capacity to import crude oil and refine it into a variety of beneficial by-products and in view of that, the CKD government will revive the Feruka Oil Refinery and associated pipelines (Beira-Mutare-Harare) within three years in office by reapplication of the same Laws of Thermodynamics used by Eng. Mbuya Muchigere for millennia in the preparation of sadza / isitshwala.

To prove that Zimbabwe has the requisite skills to design and run an oil refinery, CKD will invite crude oil fractionating systems from Zimbabwe A-Level Chemistry students and their teachers to design the crude oil processing plant in collaboration with Harare Institute of Technology, Bulawayo Polytechnic and National University of Science and Technology Departments of Applied Chemistry and Chemical Engineering to help choose the right materials to use to manufacture the system and design the requisite controls that will be used by the crude oil refinery and related plastic industry. And so the design, manufacture, installation, testing, commissioning and operation of the Feruka Oil Refinery will be done wholly by the people of Zimbabwe and not by villagers from Uzbekistan or Kazakhstan as suggested by some government officials.

Oil and Gas in Collaboration with Harare Institute of Technology,
Bulawayo Polytechnic and NUST Applied Chemistry & Chemical Enginerring Departments

Benefits of Crude Oil Processing

(i)   Jobs of refining the oil and by-products processing
(ii)   Crude oil price variations benefit more the nations that have capacity to refine
(iii)   The by-products of crude oil which include lubrication oil, plastics, tyres, roofing, nylon, pipes, industrial belts, car bodies, car batteries, enamel, refrigerants, paints, synthetic rubber among other by-products are imported mainly from South Africa as if Zimbabwe is a province of South Africa literally constitute a sizeable economy and the backbone of industry and therefore crude oil processing will benefit Zimbabwe immensely if the Feruka Oil Refinery is revived.

The key question is; do the descendants of the architects of the Great Zimbabwe need to import even tyres from other nations?

Directly, the resuscitation of the Feruka Oil Refinery will give jobs to citizens who will work at Feruka to refine oil and also afford consumers a more competitive price of fuel and by-products. Indirectly, there are spin-offs and positive ripple effects to the economy in owning the entire manufacturing of oil by-products and derivates listed herein which are currently benefiting South Africa in terms of employment generation, entrepreneurial development and general economic upliftment of the people. As can be seen from the wide product range of products and benefits of oil industry, there are far more benefits of resuscitating the Feruka Oil Refinery and associated industries than to continue importing crude oil derivatives. Dunlop is not an African corporation and the CKD government will assist Zimbabwean engineers to form a tyre manufacturing company to compete with international brands like Goodyear, Bridgestone, Yokohama, Michelin and Firestone among others and the future of Zimbabwe looks very bright under the auspices of CKD. Wezhira steel belt will beat them all if the proprietors thereof believe that they can fly.

Research on Alternative Transport Fuel

The CKD government will finance research on alternative fuel for the transport industry in order to cut dependence on fossil fuels and also save the environment. The CKD government will give guidelines on electric or alternative energy car models to Zimbabwean manufacturers to start producing as successor to the combustion engine. All carbon fuel powered equipment designed in Zimbabwe will be fitted with a carbon dioxide extractor as part of the exhaust system to guard against global pollution.

10.5   Toys and Games Industry

Central in an electronically controlled toy is a small programmable chip which can easily be programmed by undergraduate Zimbabwean students with African musicals like *Ehu-uwe Nyarara Mwana or Thula Mntwanami* and the toy industry will change forever. African children now know '*Old MacDonald had a farm*' jingle or '*Uncle Xi Chong Chi ate my dog*' more than African lullabies because African people are waiting for the 'whiteman' and the Chinese to load *Ehu-uwe Nyarara Mwana or Thula Mntwanami* in the toys. The remainder of the toy is plastic which will come from the by-products of the resuscitated Feruka Oil Refinery. The Toy and Plastic Industry will work under the mentorship of Harare Institute of Technology, Bulawayo Polytechnic and National University of Science and Technology Departments of Applied Chemistry and Chemical Engineering.

Toys and Games Industry in Collaboration with Harare Institute of Technology, Bulawayo Polytechnic and NUST.

The key question is; do the descendants of the architects of the Great Zimbabwe need to import even toys from other nations?

The CKD government will close the importation of all children's toys and games from day one in office. If the people of Zimbabwe cannot make toys for their children then they will be required to mould clay images for their children to play with, there will not be any budget for the importation of such merchandise, even donated toys will not be allowed into the country, the reason being that donated merchandise create dependence syndrome among the people. There is a lot of business in toys and other infant accessories and if the people do not own that market, that business will remain in the hands of Europe, the West and Asia where Vanhu/Abantu will be reduced to vendors of such devices who will just get a small commission and that is the dependence disease that the CKD government will eradicate. When food, clothing, toys or any other needs are donated or given freely, people will eventually lose the skills needed to fabricate or grow those human needs and when the skills vanish, whoever was donating would start selling again to very unskilled people on the basis of a monopoly deliberately created by these not so generous donor agencies!!

Who Needs To Depend On Others?

The people of Africa have human survival skills required to process or add value to their natural resources but so are the Europeans and Americans. Vanhu/Abantu have immense natural resources but others do not have as much and so those that need to depend on others are those people with no natural resources. One of the key reasons of the imperial annexation of Africa was poverty in the north and lack of natural resources (raw materials) and things were so hard that dog meat was eaten raw (hot dogs) and the moment the north annexed Africa and other third party territories things dramatically changed for Europe.

10.6   Space Science and Technology

The CKD government will embark on aerospace science and technology development through a government sponsored vehicle called Chitundumutsere-mutsere Corporation with a view to understand the outer space, galaxies and planet earth as a collective human, animal and plant habitat and help balance that ecosystem which has been seriously offset by reckless nations; through the launch of two space vehicles namely Mlimo SV 001 for medium distance space explorations followed by Kurumbi CHT2 for super long distance missions into the Galaxies of Kurumbi (Gwara raKurumbi).

The people of Africa today are a poor shadow of their founders who have been reduced to the life of survival with emphasis on the search for food and water and nothing more but CKD is introducing a new kind of leadership in Africa that will compete with any nation except in nuclear arms of savagery and barbarity and other unethical sciences for that will not be in conformity with Unhu/Ubuntu and also to prove that Vanhu/Abantu are capable of achieving any technological feat like any other people. It does not require a substantial budget to send an aerospace vehicle into orbit, all what is needed is skill and determination.

Within five (5) years of the CKD government, at least one (1) space vehicle will be launched from Thorn Hill Airbase Command and Control Centre to navigate the aerospace for research. [A space vehicle is a high heat/pressure resistant and weatherproof container propulsion powered by two, three or four liquid gas fuel cylinders at the base with high precision guidance]. Zimbabwe has human skills and natural resource metals required to send Mlimo Space Vehicle 001 on cover page and herein to planet Mars or elsewhere in collaboration with National University of Science and Technology School of Aero Space Engineering and Bulawayo Polytechnic. What is lacking in Zimbabwe is the self belief which can be measured by the number of scornful expressions meted out on this CKD campaign document. Mlimo Space Vehicle 001 will be followed by Kurumbi CHT2 for super long distance space missions in the Galaxies of Kurumbi (Gwara raKurumbi).

10.7   Software Development

(i)   Operating Softwares/Systems
Within three years of the CKD government, an operating system will be fully developed by Zimbabweans to compete with Windows, Macintosh or any other offshore operating system for the Zimbabwean and African Union market.

(ii)   Search Engines and Internet Navigation
Within three years of the CKD government, a search engine and internet navigator will be fully developed by Zimbabweans to compete with Google, Bing, Explorer, Chrome, Fire Fox or any other search engine or navigator for the Zimbabwean and African Union market.

(iii)   Application Softwares – Banking, Accounting, Air Reservations and Ticketing
Within four years of the CKD government, Zimbabwean enterprises will design banking, accounting, air ticketing and reservation systems among other applications to work on the local Operating System referenced in 10.7 (i) for the Zimbabwean and African Union market.

(iv)   Social Networks
Within three years of the CKD government, Zimbabwean enterprises will develop social networks with high tint of Unhu/Ubuntu to compete with international brands including and but limited to Facebook, Whatsapp, Youtude and Instagram.

(v)   Databases
Within four years of the CKD government, Zimbabwean enterprises will develop database systems applicable for various social, statistical, financial or industrial applications for the local and African Union market.

(vi)   Apps
Within three years of the CKD government, Zimbabwean enterprises will develop various apps for use by the Zimbabwean and African Union market.

(vii)   Anti-Viral, Anti-spy ware
Within three years of the CKD government, Zimbabwean enterprises will develop anti-viral and anti-spy ware for use by the Zimbabwean and African Union market.

(viii)   Programmable Logic Control

Within three years of the CKD government, Zimbabwean enterprises will develop programmable logic control and SCADA programs for use in Zimbabwean and African Union market to compete with global brands like Omron, Johnson Control and Allen Bradley among others.

Software Development will be done by Zimbabwean enterprises in collaboration with Solusi University, Bindura University of Science Education, National University of Science and Technology — Computers and Information Science Department and Kushinga Phikelela Technical College.

10.8   Information Communication Technology

Passive devices that include but not limited to cables, fibre optics, radio feeder cables, microwave wave guides, antennae (dipoles and directional), racks and active devices like power supplies will be locally produced within one (1) year of the CKD government for the Zimbabwean and African Union market.

Mobile phones will be produced in Zimbabwe one year after the processor target or within four years of the CKD government for Zimbabwe and the African Union market.

Telecommunications systems are easier to design for reason of standardisation of data bytes or data streams/structures (bytes, 64kb/s stream, 2.048 Mb/s, Ethernet, GSM/3G/4G/XG Mobile, SONET or SDH formats); special design attention will be given to synchronization and error correction. Active telecom devices and systems including but not limited to routers, switches, transmitters, receivers, multiplexers and test equipment will be locally produced in Zimbabwe for the Zimbabwean and African Union market within seven (7) years of the CKD government. All telecommunications systems active devices with target date of seven years will be imported without the passive devices like cables, racks, fibres optics and antennae among other passive devices after year one of the CKD government on the understanding that Zimbabwean enterprises will be manufacturing that category of equipment.

ICT Hardware Manufacturing in Collaboration with Harare Polytechnic, Kushinga Phikelela Technical College, EGU, CUZ and NUST

Computer Hardware

Computer and PLC hardware will be designed and manufactured by Zimbabwean enterprises with components supplied by the Semi-conductor manufacturing vehicle in article 10.2 within four years of the CKD government for the Zimbabwean and African Union market.

Information Communication Technology equipment will be designed and manufactured by Zimbabwean enterprises in collaboration with Harare Polytechnic, Kushinga Phikelela Technical College, Ezekiel Guti University, Catholic University of Zimbabwe Department of Information Communication Technology and National University of Science and Technology Departments of Applied Physics and Electronics.

10.9   Power Generation and Transmission Equipment

High tension and distribution electrical transformers which consist of windings, core, oil, control and monitoring sensors will with immediate effect of the CKD government be manufactured in Zimbabwe by Zimbabwean enterprises while electrical generators (fuel and hydro), electric motors which are basically electrical cable wound on laminated core and encased in a housing and solar power generation systems will have a target date of three (3) years. The technologies are simple to make and as long as Zimbabweans or Africans do not take it upon themselves to manufacture their goods and services, the suppliers from America, Europe and Asia will not come to Africa to lecture on how easy it is to manufacture such devices, but will keep on supplying goods on demand to the market and invoicing and will pray that Africans remain their customers forever.

There are so many applications or uses of the electric motor which bring a lot of business in motor design, manufacture and maintenance for the following needs to give Zimbabwe a sky limit of opportunities;

(i)   Industrial Motors for conveyor systems, elevators, escalators, moving walkways, Aircraft Passenger Boarding Bridges, Trains, crushers, vibrators, compressors, auto-mobile, industrial tools
(ii)   Toys
(iii)   Food processors, mixers, grinders, cutters
(iv)   Vacuum cleaners and extractors
(v)   Money counters, Automatic Teller Machines
(vi)   Medical centrifuges and equipment
(vii)   Robotics
(viii) Compressors, Fans and blowers
(ix)   Pumps

Power Generation and Transmission Equipment Manufacturing in Collaboration with Gweru Polytechnic, Kwekwe Polytechnic and University of Zimbabwe

Power and Generation Equipment will be manufactured by Zimbabwean enterprises in collaboration with Gweru Polytechnic, Kwekwe Polytechnic and University of Zimbabwe Electro-Mechanical Department.

10.10 Lighting Systems

Lighting systems for all applications including but not limited to airfield lighting, domestic, commercial, industrial, electronic and transport will have a target date of three (3) years of the CKD government to compete and replace product brands like Osram, Phillips, General Electric, Thorn, Alstom and Honeywell among others for the Zimbabwean and African Union market in collaboration with Harare Institute of Technology, Westgate Technical College and University of Zimbabwe Electrical Department.

Lighting Systems Manufacturing in Collaboration with Westgate Technical College, Harare Institute of Technology and University of Zimbabwe

The key question is; do the descendants of the architects of the Great Zimbabwe need to import even light bulbs from other nations?

10.11 Instruments and Sensors

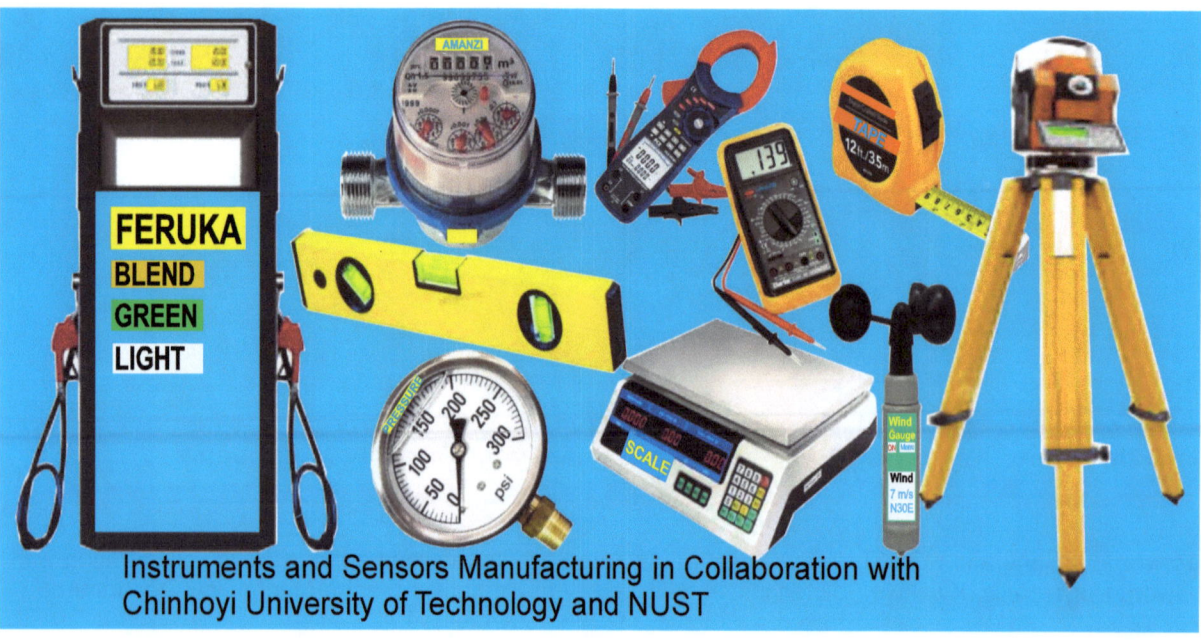

Instruments and Sensors Manufacturing in Collaboration with Chinhoyi University of Technology and NUST

(i)　Industrial Instruments and Sensors

Industrial instruments and sensors for measurement of physical phenomenon such as temperature, pressure, flow, level, voltage, current, resistance, sound, frequency, power, vibration, speed, time, inductance, capacitance, distance, angle, weight, smoke, elevation and transmitters thereof among others will be designed and manufactured in Zimbabwe within five years of the CKD government as part of the Industrial Evolution for the Zimbabwean and African Union market.

(ii)　Weather Sensing and Reporting Systems

Weather instruments for measuring humidity, precipitation, wind speed, wind direction, cloud base and visibility among other parameters will be produced by Zimbabwean enterprises within three years of the CKD government.

(iii)　Medical Equipment

The CKD government will facilitate the local design and fabrication of the following medical instruments within five years in office for Zimbabwe and African Union market; clinical manometer, stethoscope, clinical thermometers, ventilators, blood centrifuges (small motor with timer), haemodialysis machines, microscopes (just an adjustable magnifying lens), X-rays machines (which are just electromagnetic oscillators and films or display for imaging) and ultra-sound scanners/analysers among other medical equipment. These instruments are very basic to understand, design and fabricate and it is a wonder why several years after their discovery Vanhu/Abantu are not manufacturing such basic equipment.

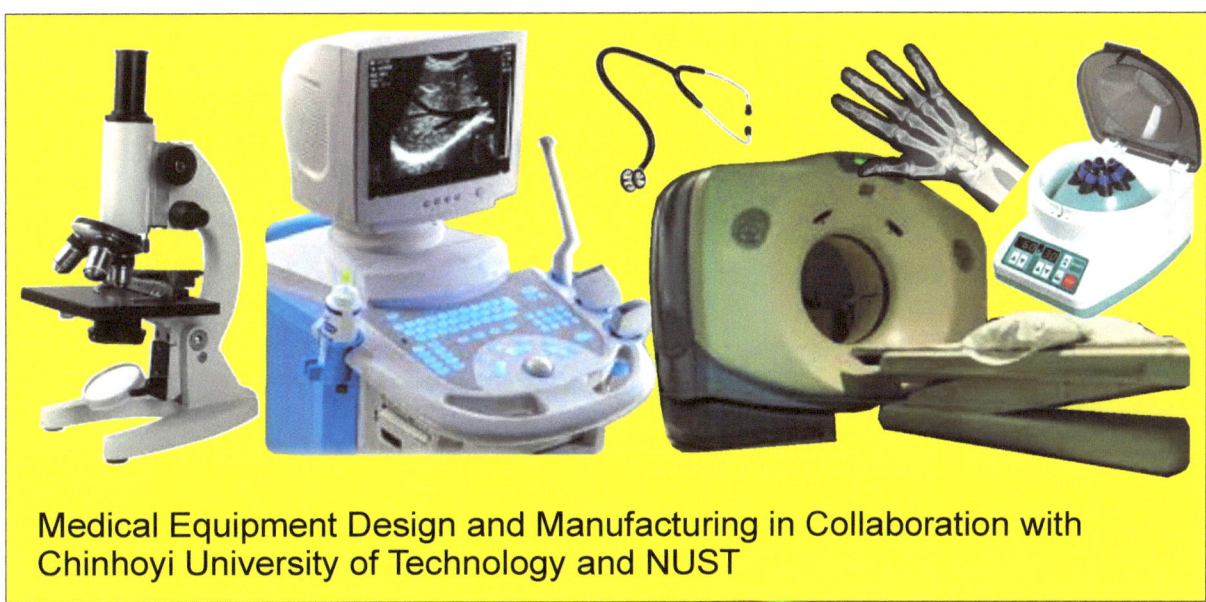

Medical Equipment Design and Manufacturing in Collaboration with Chinhoyi University of Technology and NUST

Instruments and Sensors will be manufactured by Zimbabwean enterprises in collaboration with Chinhoyi University of Technology and National University of Science and Technology Departments of Applied Physics and Electronics.

10.12　Industrial Tools and Accessories/Consumables

Zimbabwe has the second largest chrome ore reserves in the world and chromium is the key metal in most cutting tools yet the country exports raw chrome ore for other countries including India and China which are developing countries like Zimbabwe, to make tools and export back to Zimbabwe at multiple times the price of chrome ore causing Zimbabwe to lose jobs and value addition economic benefits. In view of these loses, the CKD government will ensure that industrial tools and accessories such as drilling, cutting, grinding, machining, polishing, welding, pumps, vibrators, bearings, solder, high performance alloy screw drivers and spanners will be designed and fabricated in Zimbabwe by

Zimbabwean companies within three years in office for the Zimbabwean and African Union market in collaboration with Msasa Technical College, Gwanda State University and University of Zimbabwe Metallurgy Department. No special skills are required to make screw drivers other than the knowledge of the ratio of alloy mixing to achieve a certain material of desired strength, melt and pour into the required forms, not a big deal at all.

CKD has personally observed hardworking Zimbabweans buying a tool like an electric drilling machine from Asia which broke both its drill bit and motor while drilling its first hole after which they started swearing at everyone around them, it is unimaginable how so much effort, money, time and logistics are wasted through importation of such junk equipment from Asia when Vanhu/Abantu can make better equipment. The CKD government will close the Zimbabwean market from such junk equipment, for sure.

The key question is; do the descendants of the architects of the Great Zimbabwe need to import even screw drivers and spanners from other nations?

The manufacturing of cutting tools as an example will start with choosing the correct hard alloy mixtures followed by making patterns/forms then melting of alloys to put into the forms, cooling, polishing and making insulated covers and eventually sending to the market, it is very easy to be a developed economy as Zimbabwe will shortly become.

The Great Zimbabwe has worked in metals to make tools for millennia through its engineers (mhizha) and the contemporary Zimbabwe has no justification for failing to do what the ancestors did thousands of years back, perhaps general laziness and reluctance to think can be the justification.

Industrial Tools and Accessories Manufacturing in Collaboration with Msasa Technical College, Gwanda State University and UZ Metallurgy Department

10.13 Farm Equipment

The entire African continent is like a garden capable of producing agricultural produce all year round but the people of Africa cannot make agricultural tools and equipment to use to farm this garden.

In view of the above anomaly, the CKD government will ensure that within five (5) years in office, agricultural machinery including but not limited to medium sized combine harvesters branded Jakwara/ Nhimbe 12 on cover page and herein, tractors Umlimi X01, planters, incubators and irrigation systems

Mpfula Kahina /Mvura Naya-naya 20 will be manufactured by indigenous manufacturers in collaboration with Mutare Polytechnic, Masvingo Polytechnic and Africa University for the Zimbabwean and African Union market with more emphasis on drip irrigation as water resources are getting more scarce as a result of global environmental pollution.

10.14   Mining and Earth Moving Equipment

Africa is home to every mineral known to this civilization but the same people do not make mining equipment and virtually are onlookers to the whole mining industry where Europeans, Americans and Asians bring mining equipment onto Africa, mine the minerals and export the minerals to their homes abroad while the African human species is just gazing.

In the view of people who are importing needles, Mining and Earth Moving Equipment looks complicated, intimidating, completely out of reach and unachievable target but the design and manufacture of that kind of equipment is no different from the auto mobile except in size. The manufacturing processes are the same of casting or moulding engine blocks, machining pistons and

other parts like hydraulic systems, assembling and job done, then Chigaduro GR50 will be sent to the market showrooms after which Caterpillar, CASE, Komatsu among other manufacturers will start feeling the heat of Great Zimbabwe competition. The rough diamonds from Chiadzwa among other places will be fitted onto the cutting edges of the earth drilling machines as opposed to the current raw export of rough diamonds to Asia and Europe. Crushers, smelters, gravity separators and industrial conveyors among other mining equipment will be produced by Zimbabwean enterprises within five years of the CKD government for the Zimbabwean and African Union market in collaboration with Zimbabwe School of Mining, Bulawayo Polytechnic and Gwanda State University.

10.15 Construction Equipment

Concrete mixers, cranes, compactors and vibrators among other associated equipment will be produced by Zimbabwean enterprises in collaboration with Masvingo Polytechnic, Mutare Polytechnic and Great Zimbabwe University within five years of the CKD government for the local and African Union market.

Construction Equipment Manufacturing in Collaboration with Masvingo Polytechnic, Mutare Polytechnic and Great Zimbabwe University

10.16   Audio Visual Equipment

Audio Equipment

All equipment relating to audio systems such as microphones (vibrating crystal or wafer with connection points to a mixer or amplifier), speaker (magnet and wafer), mixers (audio filters and attenuators), amplifiers (cascaded integrated circuits or transistors available from the Semi-conductor Manufacturing vehicle) will be manufactured in Zimbabwe within four years of the CKD government using the same sound engineering used for millennia on ngoma/ingun'u with manufacturers sourcing the bulk of their components from the Semi-conductor Manufacturing vehicle administered directly by the Head of State.

Cameras

A camera is made up of a focussing lens and code converters after which manufacturers start invoicing for products made *isu vanhu takangoti vavava /thina abantu silele*. The code converters will be easily available through the Semi-conductor Manufacturing Vehicle and Zimbabwean enterprises will be able to compete with international brands like Cannon, Sony, Panasonic and JVC among others. The target date for local camera manufacturing will be within four years of the CKD government for the Zimbabwean and African Union market.

Audio Visual Equipment Manufacturing in Collaboration with Harare Polytechnic and Zimbabwe Open University

Hi-fis and Televisions

Hi-fis and televisions will be produced in Zimbabwe within four years of the CKD government for the Zimbabwean and African Union market. Audio Visual equipment will be manufactured by Zimbabwean enterprises in collaboration with Harare Polytechnic and Zimbabwe Open University.

10.17   Broadcasting Equipment

Passive Devices

Feeder cables, coaxial cables, racks, attenuators, resonance cavities, antennae, loading devices among other equipment will be produced in Zimbabwe by indigenous manufacturers within one (1) year of the CKD government.

Active Devices

Transmitters, receivers, amplifiers, equalisers, encoders, decoders, mixers, video cameras, audio microphones, test equipment among other broadcasting equipment will be designed and manufactured by Zimbabwean manufacturers for Zimbabwe and African Union market within five (5) years of the CKD government. All broadcasting equipment active devices with target date of five years will be imported without the passive devices like cables, racks, fibre optics, attenuators and antennae among other passive devices after year one on the understanding that Zimbabwean enterprises will be manufacturing that category of equipment in collaboration with Bulawayo Polytechnic and Zimbabwe Open University.

10.18   Refrigeration and Air-Conditioning

Refrigeration and air-conditioning are the compressor, heat exchange and insulation and within three (3) years of the CKD government, indigenous compressor brands like Xirhami/Chando will be produced by enterprises in Zimbabwe to meet the refrigeration and air-conditioning needs of Zimbabwe and the African Union in collaboration with Masvingo Polytechnic, Mutare Polytechnic and Great Zimbabwe University.

Refrigeration and Air-Conditioning Equipment Manufacturing in Collaboration with Masvingo Polytechnic, Mutare Polytechnic and Great Zimbabwe University

10.19 People Moving Equipment

The elevator is a cage/car run by electric motor, hoist cable with safety features like open/close door controls plus over-speed guard. Elevators, escalators and moving walks will have a target date of three years, the same as the target date for the electric motor which is the key driver of such equipment. Zimbabwe will not require the services of Schindler, Kone, Mitsubishi and Otis among similar manufacturers to assemble a cage with hoist cable all the way from Germany, America or Japan which can easily be assembled at Gazaland in Highfields, Makokoba or Sakubva Green Market while Zimbabwean engineers will design the safety control programs and devices of that equipment for the Zimbabwean and African Union market in collaboration with Kubatana Technical College and Chinhoyi University of Technology.

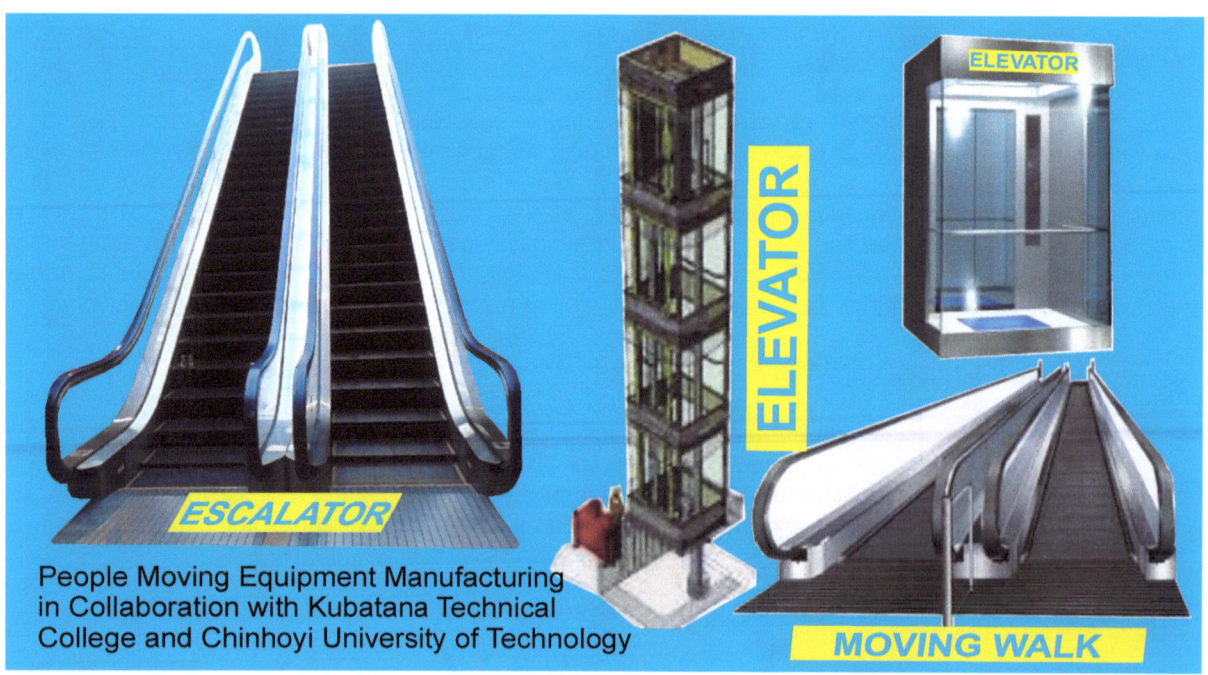

People Moving Equipment Manufacturing in Collaboration with Kubatana Technical College and Chinhoyi University of Technology

10.20   Textile Technology and Processing

Cotton farming is profitable if the economy has capacity to process cotton from ginning of raw cotton into lint then yarning or weaving sheets of textile and ultimately consumer clothing. The processing of cotton into the final consumer clothing requires tools starting from harvesters, ginneries, weavers and sewing machines, all of which are imported in Zimbabwe which makes the textile industry end products expensive when compared to other economies and this causes people to import cheaper clothing from other countries. The textile industry has numerous empowerment and job opportunities starting from farming, farm equipment manufacturing, cotton processing equipment, end product clothing design and marketing yet Zimbabwe only sits on the bottom end of the chain which has caused most farmers to abandon cotton farming in preference of other cash crops.

Textile Technology and Processing in Collaboration with Mupfure Technical College and Women University of Africa

In view of the above, Zimbabwe cotton farmers will be given the price of cotton per kilogram which is equal to their production cost, plus profit and insurance, transport to Asian, European and American markets or simply the offshore landing price of cotton lint.

The key question is; do the descendants of the architects of the Great Zimbabwe need to import even under garments from other nations or put on donated second hand clothing?

All equipment relating to the textile industry processing branded Musoni herein with the competitive edge of international brands like Brother, Juki, Singer among others will have a manufacturing target date of three (3) years after which all imports of such equipment will cease in order to support local manufacturers and the economy. On day one (1) of the CKD government before the maturity of cotton processing equipment like sewing machines, weavers and ginneries, citizens will be allowed to import processing equipment but all clothing imports will not be available for the market except fabrics whose raw material like silk is not available in Zimbabwe to give opportunities to citizens trained in clothing design and marketing to make use of their trade and clothe Zimbabwe in collaboration with Mupfure Technical College and Women University of Africa. If there are certain types of clothing designs that the market requires from off-shore, local clothing manufacturers will be required to make such designs for Zimbabwe and not continue to dole-out such business opportunities to other nations.

10.21　　　Military Hardware

Africa originated this civilization and evidence of that human development milestone is visible at Giza in Egypt and the Great Zimbabwe among other places and Africa will continue to lead in this civilian domain to encourage other nations to follow suit and shun savagery or barbarity and in that regard, the CKD government will not have any meaningful design and manufacturing targets for military hardware. The Great Zimbabwe has both natural resources and skills to make nuclear arms but what is not there among Vanhu/Abantu is the heart of a savage/barbarian which is prevalent among nuclear nations, required to design and fabricate nuclear arms of savagery or barbarism. Humans do not have horns or other body features to defend themselves but that did not mean that they would use a bigger brain to design arms of barbarity to defend themselves but are required to use the brain to discuss conflict amicably and to that regard, Africans (Vanhu/Abantu) by identity derive their name from Unhu/Ubuntu which is the human moral code of conduct and have no history of conquest or any form of barbarity and will continue to be guiltless.

And to encourage other nations to embrace civility and shun savagery or barbarity, the CKD government will lobby non-nuclear nations to impose a nuclear trade tariff on all goods and services originating from nuclear nations to the extent that nuclear arms will be an albatross not around the necks of those nations without nuclear arms of savagery and barbarity but around the necks of their maker and the nuclear trade tariff will be proportional to the number of nuclear warheads in stock; sounds like a sweet stream flowing in the hearts of peaceful nations.

10.22 Tertiary Institution Industrial Evolution Assignments

S. No.	Industrial Evolution Assignment	Institution
5.1	Small Grain Farming	Chibero, Gwebi, Rio Tinto, Mlezi, Esigodini
5.3	National Fruit Tree Roll-out	FC, BP, Mupfure Tech
10.	Manufacturing Internship	NUST
10.2	Semi-conductor Manufacturing	NUST
10.3	Small Vehicles 2.5cc, Motor Bikes and Bicycles	MSU, GwP, KwP
	Small to Medium Trucks 2-5 Tonnes	MSU, GwP, KwP
	Large Trucks, Buses, Earth Movers and Excavators	BUSE, Msasa Tech, Kubatana Tech, Westgate Tech
	High Speed Trains (Mvema)	LSU, BP,
	Passenger Airplanes 200 and 300 seaters	UZ; HP, Mupfure Tech
	Passenger Airplane Engines	UZ, HP, Mupfure Tech
	Aviation Support Systems	UZ, HP, Mupfure Tech
10.4	Oil and Gas – Resuscitation of Feruka Oil Refinery	NUST, HIT, BP
10.5	Toys and Games Industry	NUST, HIT, BP
10.6	Space Science and Technology	NUST, BP
10.7	Software – Operating Systems, search engines, internet navigators, Anti-viral, Social Networks, Apps, PLC	SU, BUSE, NUST, Kushinga P
	Applications Systems and Data Bases	SU, BUSE, NUST, Kushinga P
10.8	Information Communication Technology passive devices	HP, EGU, CUZ, NUST, Kushinga P,
	Mobiles Phones	HP, EGU, CUZ, NUST, Kushinga P
	Routers, Switches, Transmitters, Receivers and Multiplexers	HP, EGU, CUZ, NUST, Kushinga P
10.9	Power Generation and Transmission Equipment	UZ, GwP, KwP
10.10	Lighting Systems	HIT, UZ, Westgate Tech
10.11	Industrial Instruments and Sensors	CUT, NUST
	Weather Sensing and Reporting	CUT, NUST
	Medical Equipment	CUT, NUST
10.12	Industrial Tools and Accessories	GSU, UZ, Msasa Tech
10.13	Farm Equipment	MuP, MaP, AU
10.14	Mining and Earth Moving Equipment	ZSM, GSU, BP
10.15	Construction Equipment	MaP, MuP, GZU
10.16	Audio Visual Equipment and Cameras	HP, ZOU
10.17	Broadcasting Passive Equipment	BP, ZOU
	Broadcasting Active Equipment	BP, ZOU
10.18	Refrigeration and Air-Conditioning	MaP, MuP, GZU
10.19	People Moving Equipment	CUT, Kubatana Tech
10.20	Textile Technology and Processing	WUA, Mupfure Tech
11.1.11	Nutrition, Health and Medical Research	NUST, UZ, AU
11.2.4	Agriculture and Land Use	GSU, EGU, SU, AU
11.2.5	Water Development	NUST
11.2.6	Tax System	CUZ, MSU, WUA, ZOU
11.2.7	Nurturing of Entrepreneurs	All Institutions
11.2.8	Zimbabwe Marketing Corporation	SU, LSU, EGU, MSU, WUA
12.2	Environmental Protection and Research	SU, BUSE, ZOU

After the above assignments and targets are set, wonders and technology records will be made not by Harvard, Massachusetts or Cambridge but by Zimbabwean Universities from the children of the Great Zimbabwe and the future looks bright and enrolling in Zimbabwean Universities and colleges will be highly sought after and students from other nations will come to Zimbabwe in search of education.

College students will be required to make a meaningful improvement to the Zimbabwe Industrial Evolution products as precondition for graduation and students will be expected to be fully engaged with academic and research work and there will not be time for prostitution which is currently rife in colleges.

Chapter 11   Domestic Policy Issues

11.1   Political Policy Issues

11.1.1   Gun-less Society

A gun-less society is more safe for every citizen as a collective and aspiring gun owners are safer in a gun-less society than if a few of them were to be licensed to own guns. If a gun-less robber was to approach any home, just locking him outside the home and making a call to the police would not pose any problem to people. All foreign embassies will be required to keep or carry no gun anywhere in Zimbabwe and diplomatic protection will be guaranteed by the national army and police. A gun will be allowed only to be carried by a soldier on national duty to the extent that people will be very proud of the national army, not even a bank with cash-in-transit will be allowed to own or carry a gun. A citizen who arms self to rob or kill will be deemed to have signed his/her death warrant and a crack team of snipers will be deployed to effect the death shot.

In America, gun manufacturing is a formidable industry with all sorts of customers who kill or shoot at random any time while news channels would be very happy to break the news and police departments feel grateful and indebted to the gun for their jobs because without the gun there would hardly be any crime in America. American status of super power has its basis on the gun and not on philosophy and generally American culture revolves around the gun or bullet in motion picture, in the streets in day to day life, in the home and at school and if the gun is taken away from that system, everything collapses. The originators of this civilization from the depth of Africa will not sink to such depths of savagery and barbarism.

11.1.2   The National Army

The national army will be made lean to consist of about 30,000 highly trained personnel, like the seven Chinhoyi Battle veterans, with battalions named after those soldiers among other names who will fight based on modern war tactics plus a blend of African traditions of flying soldiers *vachinyangarika sehangaiwa kana zvaipisisa / uzulu enyamalala njenga mugombhane.*

11.1.3   The Police Force

The police force will be lean and will consist of about 5,000 officers, highly trained in modern policing methods with a blend of African traditions to identify criminals in crimes committed in the absence of witnesses or evidence and on that basis there will hardly be any crimes as citizens will be in the clear view of tradition which will be like a virtual closed circuit television. In fact people are committing so many crimes today to take advantage of the Roman/English/Dutch law in place which cannot decisively identify criminals in crimes committed in the absence of a witness or evidence. Under the leadership of CKD, Zimbabwe will be a crimeless state and security enterprises will be advised to invest in other businesses and such a state of crimelessness will ripple on to the reduction in the cost of insurances related to loss due to theft or fraud.

Today the police force is overstaffed and there are too many officers loitering on the roads in search of bribes or money making opportunities.

11.1.4   The Prison System (Mhosva Inoripwa / Ubadalo)

All Zimbabwean prisons will be closed by the CKD government on day one (1) with prison inmates integrated onto the job market to work from home to pay for their crimes, compensate for goods stolen, destroyed or any other inconveniences caused at double the price; one portion to the complainant and the other portion to the government as a measure to discourage crime for it does not pay and in line with the traditions of the founders of the Great Zimbabwe who did not have prisons to keep criminals in custody. The convict's salary will be deducted the penalties of crime while leaving some money for family upkeep. The justice system in Zimbabwe shall be based on the concept of Mhosva Inoripwa / Ubadalo that was in place prior to imperial annexation of Zimbabwe. Murderers have no place in this civilization and no criminal will be fed while on holiday in prison and the CKD government will not spend a penny for the upkeep of criminals. There are several reports of ex-prisoners committing crimes few minutes after being released from prison, this they do in order to go back to state sponsored holidays and CKD will put an end to sending criminals on vacation. Using the traditional crime detection system, it will take a maximum of three (3) days from time of crime report to conviction of the suspect. Penalty will escalate to three fold in cases of suspects who refuse to come open with their crimes or misdeeds.

11.1.5   The Death Penalty

Convicts in cases of murder will die after a verification process performed by tradition that indeed the person convicted for murder truly is guilty of murder, the Roman/English/Dutch law sentences people to death on the basis of probability but African tradition makes no mistake.

When the convict dies as per judgment, the state will compensate the deceased family of the victim of murder in case of loss of a breadwinner for reason of failure to protect the breadwinner among other citizens. Abolishment of the death penalty is not coming from the vulnerable citizens but from politicians with several dozens of body guards to secure their life or from foreign Government Organizations (NGOs) with special protection dispensations who are far disconnected from the vulnerability of thuggery.

11.1.6   Anti-Poaching Laws

The CKD government will not spend a penny on anti-poaching security, the national parks will not be guarded against poaching but a noose will be put in place in the form of rhino horn/ elephant tusk trading tariff around the neck of especially the Asian market among others of such commodities as long as the rhino horn and elephant tusks are still on demand in those markets. There will not be any need to play cat and mouse games with the perverts. A rhino horn or elephant tusk trading tariff will make their products uncompetitive for reason of illicit rhino horn or elephant tusk trade and if there is more business in that illicit horn trade than losing the competitiveness of their goods on the African market, then the perverts can carry on poaching. The countries with thriving business based on poached raw material will fight that illicit trade in order to survive on the global market as the rhino horn and elephant tusk trading tariffs will make their products uncompetitive, in other words economics will compel the poacher markets to whip their perverts into line in order to survive.

CKD is worried when the current government allows tourists to come to Africa to hunt and kill in the name of trophy hunting of animals like lions, leopards among other non-food wildlife, what is the objective of killing a lion? There are animals in Africa because the fore bearers lived in harmony with animals while the Europeans ate dog meat to almost extinction. The CKD government will outlaw trophy hunting in liaison with the African Union and put in measures to ensure that tourists come to Zimbabwe or Africa to view and not kill animals. What savage mindset would pride itself in the wanton killing of animals? CKD has watched on television a Caucasian female killing a leopard then started laughing and smiling as a measure of accomplishment, oh no! Some folks have serious moral issues from inquisition of the Middle Ages through slave trade, imperialism, nuclear war, sodomy and racism among other issues, they do not seem to have a moral resume.

11.1.7   Guard Against Gender Abuse

The CKD government will impose very severe penalties to men who exploit women especially those that deflower women with promises of marriage but only to renege after the damage has been done. African Culture does not allow a reckless man to steal a woman's pride and get away with it. If a man is married, the woman must be informed and she must choose to make a commitment to a married man with the full knowledge that he is married. Deflowering a maid without marriage shall attract a penalty of five (5) years of fifty percent (50%) of the income of the guilty party as compensation against shame to the parents of and the maid. If a man earns a thousand dollars income per month ($1000-00), he will compensate thirty thousand dollars ($30,000-00) in five years to make it difficult for those men who see no value in chastity of womenfolk. The recommendation to men would be marry her first if you care about her. There are many single, lonely and devastated people today for the reason that an insincere person faked care, satisfied own passion and moved on and so before such folks can abuse others, they will be compelled by the law to spell out their insincere intentions before taking others for a ride, sincerity is part and parcel of unhu/ubuntu. There is a galaxy sized cultural difference between the north and south where casual gender indulgence can be welcome by some races but in African Culture it is gender exploitation.

Eradication of Gender Infections

Before a citizen commits self to another person to the extent of going to bed (engendering), will be required to undergo medical examination and certified and avail the certificate to a partner who will sign thereon to ensure that gender infection will not pass on to the other party. If the infection is incurable, the citizen will be required by law to declare to the other party and the other party will be required to acknowledge in writing and keep a record of no objection without which the other citizen will be deemed to have failed to disclose medical condition to the other party. Infecting a spouse or partner with gender disease will be an offence punishable by a compensation of fifty percent (50%) of five annual incomes of the guilty party, gender diseases are more lethal than domestic violence. The penalty is not putting a specific value at law for the reason that to some people that specific value may seem too small and so a fraction of one's annual earnings will be serious to everyone. If a woman hangs around a lazy man, her compensation will be lazy cheap as well. The penalty will be more severe in the case of infection of terminal illness and even worse if the infection was through an act of rape. A parent raises up a child of good morals who get married only to come back home divorced, thin and terminally ill, these are key areas that CKD is studying every day from people of all walks of life crying for reason of gender abuse sometimes inflicted by politicians or legislators and these abuses will come to pass. The primary objective of these measures is to eradicate gender diseases and infections within three years of the CKD government and HIV within one generation.

11.1.8   Strategy Against Crime

The motivation for crime is not only out of necessity as a result of hunger and poverty but environment. A hungry man will steal to eat if he is sure that no one is watching or that no one will catch him after the theft. If the hungry man understands that people are watching or that he will be identified even after committing the crime, he will not choose to do the obvious stupid thing of stealing to expose self but will do the right thing, ask and thou shalt be given. In view of the above, the CKD government will use a combination of modern policing methodologies and tradition to detect criminals of crimes committed in the absence of witnesses. Suspects will not need an attorney to prove that they did not commit a crime but a determination will be done through African tradition to convict criminals even in cases of crimes committed in the absence of witnesses or evidence. Zimbabwe will reach a crimeless state where people will not lock their homes when they go out for long journeys, all what they would do is close the door so that stray animals or weather elements will not disturb the home and CKD hereby advises all those businesses with interest in security to diversify on time for it will not be necessary to pay a guard for securing a premises in a crimeless state and insurance premiums will be expected to go low to cover only for accidental damage or fire and not against loss due to theft or fraud. Prior to the imperial annexation of Zimbabwe and the subsequent administration by Roman/English/Dutch law, there were hardly any cases of crime like theft as an example for the African justice system had checks and balances against crime but upon the introduction of Roman/English/Dutch law, every aspect of morality, goodwill or trust among other virtues collapsed and in view of that logic, CKD will take the people of Zimbabwe back to the good old days.

11.1.9   Fight Against Corruption

Detail on how to deal with corruption is not revealed herein in case the perverts will try to adapt but suffice to say that teeth will gnash and that the CKD government will not have an Anti-Corruption Commission, it is waste of resources. Fighting corruption will start in kindergarten and not trying to restrain middle aged Mafia from graft. Blessed are they that cannot earn through corrupt means for the future Zimbabwe envisioned by CKD belongs to them, but for those that earn through corruption, even the little that they have shall be taken away from them, *sizakuthatha mukwenyana / tichakubata mukuwasha/mukwambo.*

11.1.10   National Registration and the Passport Office

On day one of the CKD government, the entire passport office staff from top to bottom including janitors will be retrenched and replaced by performance based employment contracts. The Passport Office building will be demolished and the land exchanged with another piece of land from another government agency to construct another cleaner building which shall work in collaboration with other satellite registration offices. The destruction of the building is a necessary step in order to erase the traumatic experience endured by citizens due to the passport service that resembled a Nazi Concentration Camp. Any satellite registration office that can issue a birth certificate, will also be entitled to process passport applications as the key requirement to a passport is a birth certificate. Unclear citizenship passports will be referred to the Central Registry.

11.1.11   National Health Policy

The CKD government will invest heavily in educating the citizens on living a healthy life through eating healthy foods and engaging in healthy habits than invest billions of dollars in building hospitals to create a nation of sick and bed ridden people. CKD has no health insurance but is assured of a good health through eating healthy foods and engaging in healthy habits. Folks like Sadzandiuraye/ Tagutapadare/ Isitshwala ngibulale are dying of overeating; food will be weighed on a scale to encourage citizens to eat responsibly. Overeating (kuzvimbirwa/ukufutelwe) is a taboo in African Culture which is believed to bring extreme poverty and is so despicable yet today almost every person is showing clear signs of overeating and associated illnesses.

(i) Research on Natural Medicine

The CKD government will put more emphasis of research on natural medicine which has no side effects which was in place before the advent of Europeans and a time table shall be put in place to phase out the dangerous pharmaceutical combos from Europe, the West and Asia some of which are commercial initiatives rather than health solutions. Within ten (10) years of the CKD government, all medicine in Zimbabwe will be naturally based, after all most diseases are from reckless mating and junk food, when that gap is closed, other fewer ailments would be easier to deal with and all pharmaceuticals and dispensaries in Zimbabwe will be dispensing natural medicine.

The CKD government will prohibit pharmaceutical corporations from testing their new drugs on the people of Zimbabwe as medical guinea pigs.

(ii) Family Planning

Before the advent of the European settlers in Africa, Vanhu/Abantu used to naturally space their births to help the mother to recover and lead a healthy life and not to suppress the size of the family as required of Africans by America and Europe similar to what was required of the Hebrews of the books of Moses by the Egyptians who were worried by the growth of the Hebrew population, they thought the Hebrews would overwhelm them and in this regard the CKD government will mobilise research resources into natural family planning and within one (1) year in office, all the artificial birth control measures will be outlawed, most of which all are war tactics against the people of Africa. Africa as big and rich as it is, cannot be told to stop growing its population when Europe's super ten nations which are smaller in natural resources to the D.R. Congo, have a population which is five times or more than the D.R. Congo.

(iii) Natural Birth

The CKD government will research on methods to improve natural birth through the birth canal without the need to use the ancient Caesarean anatomical gender mutilation which only came with the Europeans as all African births were through the birth canal without any risk to the mother or child. Africa had knowledge of such medicine and were discouraged by the imperialists without justification to result in the adaptation of Vanhu/Abantu to the uncivilised Caesarean women mutilation of reproductive health which discourages some womenfolk from starting family.

(iv)   HIV Anti-Retroviral Provision to the Innocent

The CKD government will give free and unqualified anti-retroviral support to innocent victims of HIV namely spouses, children, rape victims and work related infections and any persons outside this bracket will finance their health care in the same way that they financed the indulgence that brought the infection. People are mating recklessly with the belief that government will pay for their recklessness through taxing innocent citizens, *ngwarati dzichazvionera / ingwenya zizazibonela*. If a citizen chooses to partake in reckless attitude or lifestyle, must be ready to take responsibility of all the consequences including penalties for infecting third parties. Nutrition, health and medical research will be done in collaboration with ZINATHA, Africa University, University of Zimbabwe and National University of Science and Technology.

11.1.12   Use of Weed/ Marijuana in Medicine and Spirituality

Weed / Marijuana   Alcohol

Effects of Weed and Alcohol on User/Consumer

S. No.	Weed	Alcohol
1.	Slight impairment of judgement.	Complete impairment of judgement.
2.	Causes lung cancer if taken as inhalement.	Causes liver cirrhosis.
3.	Natural medicine for numerous ailments.	Causes sudden death when used excessively.
4.	Increased calmness.	Increased irritability.
5.	Philosophical.	Creates a noisy personality.
6.	Meditative.	Takes away human shame and brings in dog shamelessness.
7	Serene and accommodative.	Confrontational, uncompromising and abusive.

In view of the above comparison, the CKD government will legalise the use of weed/marijuana in medicine and spirituality but will make vigorous educational campaign to inform consumers of a drug called alcohol of its dangers to the liver (liver cirrhosis) and complete impairment of judgement in social life sometimes leading to instant death, at work and while travelling but will not outlaw the consumption thereof except to pregnant women (to protect the unborn child from carelessness) and to minor children. While alcohol is known to impair judgement, causing liver cirrhosis as well as creating voracious drunken rapists who are very happy to take on a 120 year old granny or a three days old infant yet it is not outlawed, but weed which makes people calmer, quieter, more reserved, philosophical and meditative with slight impairment of judgement cannot be outlawed on that basis. Founding African fathers who have inhaled mudzanga weChikonde (weed) for millennia are not extinct but have stronger descendants Vanhu/Abantu in comparison with other races. The European settlers saw the numerous positive applications of weed to African social life and abolished it on that basis among other reasons.

11.1.13 The Government

The Executive

President — One (1), elected by popular democracy.
Deputy President – Not Substantive, leader of Parliament or Chief Justice will act as president on rotational basis when the need arises.

Ministers – Twelve (12), selected by job or employment agencies through resume/ curriculum vitae.
Deputy Minister – Nil, Ministries will have very clear policies, targets and records for any citizen to take over when the need arises.
   (1)   Education, Culture and Sports (Culture is more crucial than sports)
   (2)   Finance and Economic Development
   (3)   Agriculture, Land and Local Government (there is often conflict between Agriculture and Local Government ministries over land and merging them in one ministry with one coherent policy will solve the problem)
   (4)   Health and Nutrition (Major health problems today are ingested as 'food' like animal fat, excessive alcohol and processed sugar as more people are eating poisons for reason of ignorance of nutrition)
   (5)   Energy, Transport and Water Development
   (6)   Industry, Mining and Trade (Mining will fall under Industry and Trade to set the conditions of exports of mining as finished products only and not raw materials or raw pure metals)

(7)   Environment, Wildlife and Tourism (Without wildlife African Culture and value system will collapse including the crucial totems and so when African people allow the totemless north to kill wildlife, it is being very short-sighted)

(8)   Defence

(9)   Justice and Home Security (Policing will work in close liaison with Justice System to ensure that no citizen rights are infringed).

(10)   State Security and Information (Information is security)

(11)   Foreign Affairs

(12)   Human Resources, Public Works and Social Welfare (Labour sounds like Slave Trade labour)

Gender equality, indigenization, equal opportunities for all citizens and economic empowerment will be underlying themes in government policies and not separate or standalone ministries. Key in women empowerment is education.

(i) Humility of the Leader

Today's leaders are gods which live in splendour, travel by first class service, eat food grown in paradise and who often go to outer space for holiday while the subjects live in abject poverty in which case the leader finds it difficult to mingle freely with hungry and discontented subjects. The leader therefore invests heavily in body guards and secured motorcades. CKD will live with the people, eating what the people eat, drinking what the people drink and experiencing all the trials and tribulations of the people to the extent of taking a walk in the neighbourhoods where the subjects live without even a body guard, why would the leader be so numb-scared of his subjects? A gun-less society as envisioned by CKD will assure all citizens of peace and security. CKD will establish a close relationship with the citizens and try to live freely among the people for it is better to live freely among the citizens with some aspect of security risk than to live in a risk free security dog kernel like the American president with no breath of freedom.

(ii) Presidential Residence – The State House

CKD will not inhabit the same residence used by the imperialists but will live among the people in tents (*mumisasa)* on rotational basis; two weeks in Bulilima, another two weeks in Zhombe, another two weeks in Dotito, another two weeks in Chilonga, another two weeks in Nyamaropa, another two weeks in Benzi, another two weeks in Chikuku, another two weeks in Chirinda until year-end and during those stays, bore-holes will be sunk and irrigation systems built including homes for the village orphans and the widowed.

(iii) Remuneration of the President

It is an honour to be captain of the Great Zimbabwe and that in itself is the reward and for that reason CKD will not draw a salary from the fiscus for no galaxy of silver and gold will be greater or more rewarding than being captain of the Great Zimbabwe plus an annual vacation in Mabweadziva/ Matonjeni/Njelele or Mt Nyangani. If drawing no salary is added onto living in tents among the people and not in state house and dressed in modest traditional attire portrayed on cover page, CKD will be the most modest Head of State in the human civilization.

(iv)   Parliament and the Depoliticisation of Zimbabwe

The selection of Zimbabwean citizens into parliament will be modelled along the entry qualifications of African Dare/Dale which was through a record of outstanding achievements in works of virtue, leadership skills and expertise where renowned warriors, hunters, black smiths, farmers, medical experts among others were straight candidates of parliament and not through connections to the leader. CKD is not a politician for the reason that citizens of the world are tired and disappointed by a human species called politicians for their insincerity and blatant lies be it in America, Mexico, Greece and

Zimbabwe among other places. Democracy is extinct for it has been overtaken by money and greed as voters are manipulated by money and propaganda to vote so and so into office, it is the money that is selecting politicians and not the founding principles of democracy. Democracy is as extinct as monarchies of the Middle Ages. The current polity in Zimbabwe provides for the formation of political parties for politicians to canvass for support in order to win election but the system is fraught with many problems which include corruption, vote buying, intimidation, cheating at the ballot box which results not in the election of the best leader but the best fraudster and upon election, CKD will dissolve the existing parliament and appoint a new parliament based on the selection methodology detailed below after which the political parties finance act will become null and void whose monetary budget will be used to develop the irrigation systems among other infrastructure in the communities where people live.

Selection Methodology of Parliament

A citizen will not need a political party or a campaign budget in order to be elected Member of Parliament, however political parties will not be outlawed but will be worthless and inconsequential groupings. A parliament consisting of experts in their respective fields will produce extraordinary feats for Zimbabwe and naturally citizens will have respect for parliament. All Members of Parliament shall be selected from Zimbabweans of forty (40) years and above who have dutifully and faithfully served Zimbabwe in the capacity of;

(a) War Veterans, War Collaborators, Detainees and Restrictees
(b) Professionals – artisans, sculptors, ex-civil servants, private sector (MP Dominic Benhura)
(c) Economists (MPs Dr Bernard Chidzero, Dr Kombo Moyana, Eric Bloch, John Robertson)
(d) Authors (MPs Patrick Chakaipa, Charles Mungoshi, Tsitsi Dangarembga, Aaron Chiundura Moyo, Chenjerai Hove, Pathisa Nyathi)
(e) Academics and Researchers (MP Profs Walter Kamba, Solomon Mutsvairo, Phineas Makhurane, Christopher Chetsanga)
(f) Master Farmers
(g) Specialist Traditional Midwifes and Medical Practitioners (MP Dr. Solomon Guramatunhu)
(h) Traditional Leaders (MP Chief Rekai Tangwena)
(i) Traditional Healers (MP Prof Gordon Chavhunduka)
(j) Acclaimed Soldiers (MPs Lookout Masuku, Vitalis Zvinavashe, Dumiso Dabengwa, Sheba Tavarwisa)
(k) Artists (MPs Susan Chenjerai, Safiriyo Madzikatire, Fanyana Dube, Solomon Skuza, Jesesi Mungoshi, Simon Chimbetu, Robson Banda, Leonard Dembo, Marshall Munhumumwe, Ketai Muchawaya, Knowledge Kunenyati, Dumisani Maraire, Ephat Mujuru, Paul Matavire, John Chibadura, Patrick Mukwamba, Oliver Mutukudzi, Thomas Mapfumo, Stella Chiweshe, Lovemore Majaivana, Nicholas Zakaria, Alick Macheso, Cont Mhlanga, Raisedon Baya)
(l) Sportspersons (MPs George Shaya, David Mandigora, Stanley Ndunduma, Shakeman Tauro, Stanford Mutizwa, James Takavada, Moses Chunga, Willard Khumalo, Mercedes Sibanda, Madinda/Adam/Peter Ndlovu, Tendai Chimusasa, Byron Black, Felix Tangawarima)

Selection Criteria

Any person listed or top in the above categories will make a straight walk to parliament without any campaign for they have served Zimbabwe all their lives and do not need to convince any person to vote them to parliament and CKD is looking forward to citizens who will say so and so from the above list has not served Zimbabwe to warrant a straight walk to parliament. A database consisting of citizens who have served Zimbabwe along the itemised categories among others will be compiled and the top one hundred and fifty (150) will constitute parliament. The position of a citizen in the achievers' database will depend on the number of years of service and accolades of excellence.

A number of the current Members of Parliament elected by popular vote have largely no skills or special leadership attributes and have not satisfactorily served Zimbabwe and cannot therefore lead anyone in any field or trade. A citizen must serve Zimbabwe first before aspiring to lead and not the other way round. In the past Zimbabwe has experienced junior Members of Parliament walking into parliament straight from polytechnic with no clue on any subject matter and with no service to the nation and such junior candidates have abandoned parliament to become taxi drivers in Europe with severely damaging implications to the stature of parliament as a worthless enterprise. The current popular selection of Members of Parliament excludes genuine leaders on the basis that the current selection process is too base or savage to engage and most genuine leaders have no resources to sustain a popular election campaign where vote buying is key to winning an election. Member of Parliament (Mudare/Umdale) performance will be evaluated from the implementation of constituency projects (irrigation schemes, industrial parks, schools, people and constituency development). Member of Parliament will live in the constituency and will require permission from the leader of parliament to leave the constituency during working hours and parliamentary debates will be by video conference in the presence of ordinary citizens to create the virtual all inclusive African dare/dale and MPs will use public transport until the maturity of Injiba and Ngwarati Zimbabwean car brands.

Key decisions in parliament will be made by quality consensus and not by quantity popular vote where a good idea proposed and supported by a minority will win the day by consensus or logic. In the absence of political parties, there will be no need for people to be persuaded or coerced to attend political rallies or meetings for that would be waste of the much needed production time required in the Zimbabwe Industrial Evolution, people would be working productively in overdrive to meet the CKD Industrial Evolution targets and there will not be any time for political rallies, sloganeering and politics in general and so the business of elections or voting someone into parliament will be unpaid work and an unnecessary energy expenditure. In Greece, the ancestor of democracy, people go to elections to say 'No' to one issue but the politicians will do the opposite, so why waste time in the ballot box? And so the CKD slogan is 'Forward with Zimbabwe', 'Forward with Me', you and not CKD nor anyone else (Pamberi Neni/ Pambili Nami).

(v)   Appointment of Public Servant/ Minister/ Councillor

Ministers / councillors will be selected from competent and qualified Zimbabwean citizens by Curriculum Vitae from Zimbabwean professionals on contract basis who are not Members of Parliament, traditional leaders or priests by way of public interviews administered by at least three private job placement agencies who will shortlist to the president at least five successful candidates for the Head of State to pick one and give a contract with expectations or benchmarks and a budget. There will be no room for recycling failed government officials.

The office of a Minister or Councillor becomes vacant if;

(a) the incumbent fails the expectations or benchmarks of the employment contract, is presumed resigned or fired automatically from office;
(b) the incumbent commits any crime while in office.

Minister's Automatic Resignation

Example 1) Minister of Health and Nutrition
In the Contract of Employment for Minister of Health and Nutrition, the key expectations would be;

* Average time taken to attend to a patient at a hospital, clinic or emergency.
* Child mortality
* Rate of outbreak of Infectious Diseases
* Average mortality due to Infectious Diseases outbreaks
* Rate of spread of Infectious Diseases
* Obese population

Example 2) Minister of Justice and Home Security
In the Contract of Employment for Minister of Justice and Home Security, the key expectations would be;

* Crime rate
* Police response time to reported crime
* Turn around time from commission of crime to conviction

An autonomous Statistical Department will collect meticulously information on the above expectations nationally and the statistics will be displayed on public Electronic Boards or news bulletins on the performance of government. A red tag against a public servant or minister means that performance was below expectation for two consecutive quarters and the incumbent is deemed resigned or fired from employment and automatically adverts will be broadcasted inviting interested citizens to submit resumes or applications to fill-up the vacancy. Picking the entire government ministers and councillors from the ordinary citizens outside the political establishment will be the zenith of power to the people and will start in the Great Zimbabwe.

(vi)   Public Sector Salaries and Transport

The CKD government will abolish the opulent job positions in the public sector that include but not limited to Chief Executive Officer, Chief Operations Officer, Managing Director, General Manager and replace them with a hierarchy that starts with a team leader or coordinator among other modest job titles at the top followed by non-opulent and modest titles. It was observed that once a person is given the Chief Executive Officer or managing director post, the only sure thing that the position holder will think of is a six figure salary to suit the post without even producing one commodity to put on the market. Public sector salaries will not be fixed but will depend on the business performance of the organization. The salary ratio between the highest paid worker and the lowest paid worker shall not exceed eight (8) meaning that if the lowest paid worker earns $500, the highest paid worker cannot be paid more than $4000, [Today that ratio is as high as two thousand five hundred (2500) and unacceptable lack of order/ normalcy]. Any public servant who is earning or has earned more than the ratio of eight prescribed herein will be required to make good of the excess, 'nokuti munyika maita nhuta / umhlaba sungcweli ongqingili'. NSSA managers among other public servants who have earned salaries in excess of forty thousand (40,000) dollars when pensioners get forty (40) dollars will pay back. All ministers, directors (team leaders) and Members of Parliament will use public transport in discharging their duties to ensure cost savings that will be required to finance initial industrial research and prototype designs required in the Zimbabwe Industrial Evolution and also to ensure that senior government officers feel the trials and tribulations of the ordinary people in the delivery of service of public infrastructure, the more government officers feel the pain of a dilapidated infrastructure, the harder they will work on infrastructure development. People will understand that being a minister is no longer some access to privileges but an opportunity to serve the Great Zimbabwe. Senior government workers may be considered for transport when Zimbabwean brands of vehicles like Injiba or Ngwarati series mature as reward of success.

(vii)   Traditional Leaders

Mindful of the fact that the Liberation Struggle against imperialism was started, coordinated and led by priests (masvikiro/amadlozi) and traditional leaders who were made up of but not limited to Mapondera, Mashayamombe, Mashonganyika, Chitekedza, Chingaira, Chikomba, Gwabayana, Mangwende and Seke who were killed in battle, captured, executed, imprisoned and humiliated by the imperialists for fighting to defend their land, subjects and African value system but when Uhuru came in 1980, it came without the pre-colonial jurisdiction, land and responsibilities of traditional leaders. In view of the role played by the traditional leaders, the CKD government will restore to the traditional leaders their pre-colonial jurisdiction to preserve African Culture and value system. The senior traditional leaders will legally have the same status as a high court judge, the other leaders will have the status of magistrates.

viii)   The Justice System (Mhosva Inoripwa / Ubadalo Concept)

Upon repeal of the imperial Roman/English/Dutch law that executed and mutilated Mlimo, Nehanda, and

Kaguvi among other African heroes for defending their land and the rights of their children, a Zimbabwean constitution shall be enacted based on traditional justice system with incorporation of traditional leaders to assume their original cultural jurisdiction to preserve African Culture which is on the verge of extinction against the current global trend of growing corruption, greed or general moral decadence, lack of sincerity and trust, rise in hypocrisy among humankind and rise in poverty among the ordinary people. The basis of the Justice System shall be compensation (Mhosva Inoripwa / Ubadalo Concept) and not imprisonment.

Use of Attorney in Court or Property Transfer

Attorney in Court

Upon the repeal of Roman/English/Dutch law inherent in the current Zimbabwe Constitution, a new simple unambiguous law understandable by ordinary people with no need of a legal expert to interpret and available in all languages of Zimbabwe that combines modernity and African traditions shall be enacted and that law will not require the services of an attorney which is an unnecessary expense and overhead to the Zimbabwe justice system. Cases will be handled in accordance with African traditions to re-enact the African Dare/Dale where the complainant will lay down issues that require adjudication by the court followed by the accused being required to testify guilt or otherwise. In case of otherwise, the law will use African tradition of identifying criminals of crimes committed in the absence of witness, evidence or where the accused is refusing responsibility for crimes committed. Fighting corruption and crime now requires extraordinary measures. An attorney who was nowhere near the crime scene when the crime was committed cannot be a key official in the justice delivery system, on what basis?

Deed of Property Transfer

In cases of property sales and transfer of deeds between parties, the Deeds Office shall keep a faithful database of Zimbabwean properties and their history which will be availed to aspiring buyers and the Deeds Office will facilitate transfer of property from one owner to the other without need to pay an attorney any amount of money to facilitate the deed of transfer whose fee is absent in African Culture.

(ix)   Rape Offences

The current methods used to punish convicted rapists are not prohibitive as more women continue to be raped. The CKD government will devise a cocktail of measures and procedures that will make rapists fear even dating women let alone rape them or cause rapists to develop allergy to women. Victims of rape will be compensated by the convicted party the equivalence of fifty (50%) percent of ten annual incomes. In case of gender disease infection caused by the act of rape or if the convict is a low income earner, the penalty will be higher, locking the criminal in jail on free state food and accommodation is like congratulatory party. The castration of rapists being lobbied by the Zimbabwean Senate is lack of maturity, civility and education, there is a smarter way to discourage people from committing rape without gender mutilation.

11.2   Socio-Economic Policy Issues

11.2.1 Unhu/Ubuntu

Unhu/Ubuntu is the central theme in African Culture which was taught in the family and community but family and community have systematically broken down due to urbanization, modernization and migration and it has become necessary for Unhu/Ubuntu to be taught at national level. The CKD government will through **engagement and enticement**, require young men and women to maintain their chastity until marriage and if they cannot meet that requirement, they will be free to marry at 18 years of age while still in school but first they will be educated seriously about marriage that it is a lifetime commitment and that it will be unacceptable for a young man to leave his spouse on the basis of the aging process for that will be unacceptable gender abuse. Divorce has existed in African Culture necessitated by serious issues but not as a result of the aging process or loss of income of any of the parties to a marriage and those traditions will continue by disallowing citizens to exploit others. When young men and women marry, the father will pay lobola and all accommodation until the young couple can sustain themselves and at college the government will provide marriage quarters for married students but what the CKD government will not accept is the exploitation of women by men who try short stints of gender indulgence for the reason that there is no woman in this civilization who dreams of just satisfying another man's passion without any mutual long term commitment. Educating the girl child was one of the greatest achievements of Zimbabwe education system but the girl child has broken immoral records at colleges in her casual approach to gender interaction by reckless mating.

The girl child (*mukunda akundwa neunhu / udade ulobuntu*) has run riot with immorality and that is nullifying the milestones and achievements made in education where the educated citizens are dying of gender diseases such as cervical cancer and HIV-AIDS after so much investment in education. *Umhandara noujaya unofanira kudadisa, kwete kuti vana vanoita mhuka vabereki nevatungamiri takangoti tuzu / Ukubaindoda nomainkazana enhle kufanele kisinike uzabuzabu haikona kube njenge nyamazana zegangeni.* The CKD government will create a society that rewards diligence and sincerity so that no-one will be tempted into perversion. The family which is the building block of a civilization is under threat as issues previously available only in a marriage are now freely available even to minor children as moral decadence takes a toll on humanity. *Umhandara noujaya wemunhu haupereri musango sowembudzi/ Ukubaijaha noma intombi hakuanepelele egangeni njenge mbuzi. Umhandara unopembererwa nechimanda-manda/chishava nemadzinza maviri* and therefore *mukunda/udade* cannot casually throw away such a value system or philosophy in the bush like that.

The CKD government will put in measures to encourage chastity among children like availing more cheap educational allowances to moral and responsible children and student loans will be vetted along the lines of morality and the same will apply to the job market over and above crime or police clearance, a citizen will declare a moral report for other citizens to analyse before appointment, there will be a reward for goodliness. CKD observes that the sluts and thugs are doing very well in life while the moral and innocent people are singing blues for refusing to bend their principles in search of wealth, as a result of global rise in corruption and perversion.

At university the CKD government will provide family accommodation to married students plus extra allowances for children upkeep, the Great Zimbabwe requires more citizens especially young ones and there must never be a single case of abortion necessitated by failure by the young parents to fend for the child. African children will return to the morality of olden days where they will be permitted to go out during the night to play and listen to folklore in the community without any fear or suspicion of them playing mischief. Any elder/adult will be authorised at law to exert spot discipline to any misbehaving child in the vicinity to create scenarios of virtual fathers and mothers everywhere the children go. The task of children morality shall be CKD's personal project and all the Zimbabwean parents will be entitled to point their fingers at CKD even if only one child errs. There seem to be a convergence between human culture and dog culture (*umbwa/ unja*) into some hybrid nameless culture more inclined to dog culture than humanity.

Guard Against Girl Abuse by Sugar Daddies

The CKD government will put in place a series of punitive measures to suck-out the sugar from sugar daddies which they use to attract young girls. Special intelligence teams will be deployed around schools, communities and socialising places to extract information on the menace of sugar daddies in society through informants who will include monitored girls to ensure complete eradication or extinction of sugar daddies within year 1 of the CKD government and recreate the elders of the 1950s and beyond and not the current perverts. After the eradication of the sugar daddy human species, fathers and mothers of young children will have peace of mind that their children are very safe wherever they are.

11.2.2   Abortion

The CKD government will allow without hindrance all women who were aborted by their mothers during gestation to abort their pregnancies at any stage should they feel like; at one month or even after nine months and in this regard the government will provide free medicine for side effects, free hospital admission and post abortion specialist consultation fees, pre and post abortion expenses will be fully covered. If a woman who was not aborted by her mother terminates pregnancy, the CKD government justice system will without fail abort her from this planet. The CKD government will not allow the immoral perverts to flash *Unhu Wedu /Ubuntu Wethu* down the drain under the illusion of female liberty. If there was a way to identify or distinguish future abortion lobbyists during gestation, the CKD government would facilitate the termination of such pregnancies and stop nourishing such little perverts so that in the future there will not be anyone lobbying for abortion which usually terminates the life of little angels and leaving out the future pro-abortion perverts to grow freely to become adults so as to terminate the good offspring, the travesty and injustice of life! *Nhunzvatunzva ndidzo dzinorarama / Labobahlahlimteto kukanya bapilile.*

Male Accomplice to Abortion

The CKD government will directly attach a male accomplice to every case of abortion in the form of a male who is party to the pregnancy who directly schemes abortion with his partner or indirectly in the form of a male who rejects responsibility for the pregnancy in which he is party or a medical practitioner or any other person who provides the accessories to effect an abortion, teeth of the perverts will gnash. Eye for an eye will not make the world blind but will educate the would-be eye taker of the significance of another citizen's eye that it is equal to own eye.

11.2.3   Sodomy

Gushungo did exceptionally well on the issue of sodomy especially the wars that he fought against the very rich and powerful international sodomite lobbyists who tried to export sodomy to Unhu/Ubuntu continent, there he fought like a Great Zimbabwe warrior and CKD will neither add nor subtract to that effort.

11.2.4   Agriculture and Land Use

The CKD government will finance research on natural and organic agriculture in collaboration with Ezekiel Guti University, Gwanda State University, Solusi University, Africa University and University of Zimbabwe to foster a better diet and quality food including saving the environment for the reason that most African food cereals and vegetables (*nyivhi/lude, tsine/mbuya, derere/delele, mowa*) require no pesticides and are naturally resistant to pests, diseases and that there are far more negatives to the ecosystem consisting of people, animals and environment than positives derived from the use of pesticides. CKD's favourite green *nyivhi/lude* will be available throughout the whole year and not the seasonal it is this day. While it may be justifiable for colder climates in the northern hemisphere to make artificial food but not in Africa where land is huge with substantial sunshine to support the most natural agriculture.

(1) The CKD government will make it mandatory for all farmers in Zimbabwe to farm drought resistant and more nutritive small grain cereals (sorghum and millet) on 25% of all arable land. Most perceived droughts today may be normal seasons with low harvest as a result of trying to force northern hemisphere climate crop varieties like maize corn and wheat on African savannah.

(2) The CKD government will develop extensively drip irrigation equipment and deploy to all regions in Zimbabwe as part of the Industrial Evolution to create two farming seasons between August and April with water reservoirs for each household to enable Zimbabwe to become an exporting food basket.

(3) The CKD government will make research on long term effects of genetic modification of food and their effects on people, animals and the ecosystem.

(4) Fattening of livestock or poultry will be outlawed for the reason that animal fat is a poison called cholesterol and no one will be allowed to make millions of wealth from selling or growing that poison. Farmers will be trained on how to harvest hay in the field drains for livestock feed and how to store enough stockfeed capable of sustaining livestock for one (1) year.

(5) Poultry and animal farmers will be prohibited from accelerated production of poultry and animals by use of growth hormones in stockfeed to reduce the natural life cycle of poultry from minimum six (6) months to six (6) weeks or less as that has an impact of reducing the human health or life cycle of the consumers and cause premature adulthood or aging process. Early greying of hair and early start of adulthood in humans is partly a result of growth hormones used in animal feed.

(6) The CKD government will not compensate former commercial farmers for land acquisition but will compensate for all equipment and developments made on the farms then debit the commercial farmers for unauthorized use of Zimbabwe farm land equivalent to farm size (ha) x number of years of use x yield per hectare (tonnes) x average produce price per tonne. If compensation is credit, the government will pay the farmer and in case of debt, the farmer will compensate the government of Zimbabwe.

Land Title Deed

The farm land of Zimbabwe consisting of communal and commercial farm land will remain state land usable by any citizen through land lease and not deed of transfer and no citizen or any third party shall claim ownership of that land through title deed. Title to Zimbabwe farm land by deed of transfer has serious ramifications to the people which will classify Zimbabweans into landlords and peasants similar to European Middle Ages which necessitated serious revolutions, cannot be allowed to stand. In fact, the Zimbabwe farm land belongs to the fore bearers and the present generation is entitled to do two things; (1) work the land to sustain the children and (2) pass on the land to the next generation when the present generation expires and strictly transfer of land by deed is out of the question. Multiple farm holders will lose all the land under their lease for lack of sincerity and good will. The CKD government will redistribute all underutilised land to Zimbabwean farming graduates who were trained in the Zimbabwe agricultural colleges which include but not limited to Chibero, Gwebi, Mlezi, Rio Tinto, Esigodini and Zimbabwe universities to ensure useful and informed utilisation of land in order to secure the required food reserve. Any underutilised land due to neglect, lack of skills or multiple allocations will be repossessed by the CKD government. The tradition of supplicating for rains every spring at Mabweadziva/Matonjeni/Njelele will be revived at national level as done by the fore bearers and will be led by the Head of State.

11.2.5 Clean Water for Citizens and Urban Rates

Proper industrial waste management will be put in place in collaboration with Solusi University and National University of Science and Technology to address the problems of the cost of purification and quality of water as most problems in Zimbabwe are created so as to be solved like deliberately spoiling clothing with used oil and then start borrowing money to buy soap! The urban councils are too large and expensive to rate payers and will therefore be trimmed to remove that burden from rate payers.

The CKD government will train citizens on how to handle litter in order to reduce the number of times that garbage is disposed with a net effect of reducing monthly cost of rates. The urban councils will be required to enact bylaws that make it an offence to throw litter in undesignated areas and failure of which will attract either a monetary penalty to be used to clean the same polluted environment or violators will be required to do community service to clean the polluted areas with the expectation that citizens will evolve and adapt to proper sanitary awareness. In cases or areas where councils are not providing services for any reason, there will be no justification for councils to collect rates for doing nothing like they are doing today, life of the citizens will be easy and cheap in the time of the CKD government and thereafter. In the scheme of Industrialised Zimbabwe, there will be no janitor positions to perform dirty work for other privileged citizens, it will be the duty of all citizens to keep Zimbabwe or their homes clean without anticipating a third class citizen to come and do the dirty and demeaning job and if society remains like that, CKD will consider his initiative a failure. In line with African tradition, the business of packaging and trading drinking water will be done at no profit but will allow for equipment replacement costs and salaries of workers.

11.2.6   The Tax System

National revenue is expected to grow substantially as a result of the Zimbabwe Industrial Evolution, more companies will be doing business, more people will be employed, more merchandise will move on the Zimbabwe and African markets and in view of such development, income tax for individuals, value added tax (VAT) and corporate taxes will be reduced in accordance with the following time table:

Tax	Current Tax Level	Tax at Yr 3	Tax at Yr 6	Tax at Yr 9
Value Added Tax	15 %	12.5 %	10 %	7.5%
Income Tax	Variable (V)	V-2.5%	V-5%	V-7.5%
Corporate Tax	Variable (V)	V-2.5%	V-5%	V-7.5%

Cumulative Value Added Tax will be reviewed in collaboration with Catholic University of Zimbabwe, Midlands State University, Women University of Africa and Zimbabwe Open University in order to further reduce the tax burden on citizens with a target of making Zimbabwe the lowest taxed nation in the world.

11.2.7   Early Nurturing of Entrepreneurs

The CKD government will pay for tertiary education projects or researches which seek to develop business persons straight from college who will be job creators rather than job seekers. All final year projects will be required to be marketable businesses with government assistance on revolving fund basis to create entrepreneurs but non-final year projects by other grades will not be barred from government support.

11.2.8   Zimbabwe Marketing Corporation

The CKD government will create a marketing vehicle to help market goods and services especially of up-starting companies to remove the burden of marketing and logistics by scouting for niche markets in Zimbabwe and the African Union.

Zimbabwe Marketing will work in collaboration with Solusi University, Ezekiel Guti University, Midlands State University, Lupane State University and Women University of Africa to formulate sound marketing and branding strategies for the Zimbabwe Industrial Evolution products.

Chapter 12   Foreign Policy Issues

12.1   Nuclear Trade Tariff

Anti-nuclear proliferation tariff will be levied on goods and services produced by nations with nuclear warheads (USA, Russia, UK, France, China, Israel, North Korea, India and Pakistan). The CKD government will not finance the economic prosperity of nuclear savagery or barbarism but will lobby non-nuclear nations to effect the nuclear trade tariff. The nuclear arms will be an albatross not on the necks of those nations without nuclear arms of war but on the necks of the makers of nuclear arms of barbarism. Nuclear nations must be smartly disarmed in a civilized world for the reason that as the world population puts pressure on the available resources, there will be gnashing of teeth especially in the fingernail sized Europe which has for centuries lived large on third party resources which may then be tempted to use nuclear arms of savagery to annex third party territory and avert the hunger of the 'hot dog' days that prompted imperialism. Nuclear arms are a menace especially to those nations without such arms but the answer is not to arm self but to disarm the nuclear savages smartly. CKD is bringing in a new kind of African leadership and it is not going to be business as usual in north-south relations.

The nuclear and racism tariffs are extra-ordinary measures taken in a brutal world in order to survive bearing in mind that slave masters, imperialists, racists and nuclear nations have been consistently one people while the victims to all these vices on the other side have been consistently one people. **The UN cannot be depended upon as an umbrella body that can protect the people of colour from world brutality for the reason that the UN is an international joke.**

12.2   Environmental Pollution Tariff

The CKD government will lobby the AU to impose a trade tariff on all goods and services originating from countries whose industries emit more carbon dioxide (CO_2) than they can sink or those countries that deal in hardwoods which is causing massive deforestation of pristine forests of 1000 yrs old trees to encourage nations to protect the environment which is a shared habitat and whose pollution would affect all. The business of persuading nations to protect the environment will not work but economic sanctions will do the job by making all goods and services made by global pollution more costly and uncompetitive. Environmental research will be done in collaboration with Solusi University, Bindura University of Science Education and Zimbabwe Open University.

12.3   Economic Approach to Racism

The CKD government will lobby African nations at African Union level to impose a landing racism tariff on all goods and services produced by countries with known incidents of racism in sport, social life or at work places in order to eradicate racism, the current piecemeal measures are not seriously addressing the issue of racism and will not solve the problem. Folks who throw bananas at others while sounding monkey chants will learn hard that by doing so they are throwing their national economies into the abyss.

12.4   The African Union

The CKD government will lobby African states for the creation of a more united political and economic African Union which will unify African member state armies into battalions of the African Union ready for deployment where need arise without room for the invasion of Africa by foreign states as done by NATO over Libya and any foreign forces present especially in West Africa will be sent back to their imperial homelands. The African Union Army (AUA) will have battalions or brigades equal to the member states and will for example consist of AUA – Nigerian Battalion, AUA – Egyptian Battalion, AUA – Great Zimbabwe Battalion among other African battalions with African heads of state sitting as the Joint Commanders in Chief who will convene when the need arise to deploy the five (5) million active soldiers to annihilate enemy perverts and protect the people from external brutality and savagery such as one that murdered and mutilated Muammar Gaddafi and caused the chaos that ensued in Libya. Moreover, military coups in Africa will be very difficult to sustain in case of one battalion in any African country assuming power by overthrowing a Head of State who also will be a Joint Commander in Chief of the larger African Union Army comprising of five million active soldiers.

The African economic union will allow for member states to support African enterprises to design and manufacture goods required by Africa in order to wholly own the entire African market as envisioned by this CKD campaign document where member states would produce quotas proportional to their natural resources and skills to economically empower the people of Africa who were prejudiced by slave trade and imperialism bearing in mind that the key objective of imperialism was to own the African land, natural resources, market and subjugate Vanhu/Abantu for a very long time.

12.5   United Nations Reform

The CKD government will whip African Union members to lobby for UN Reform within one (1) year to allow for equal powers and privileges to **ALL MEMBER STATES** especially but not limited to the veto power or any other attribute of permanent Security Council membership otherwise all AU members will cease to be members of the United Nations to effectively reduce the UN to the level of the Union of Neo-Nazis, Fascists, Ku Klux, Mafia, Zionists, racist Skinheads and unprintable religious extremists less civilized than the Middle Ages *zvakangosangana /kuhlangene* kuNew York UN Headquarters while they gather to discuss their special privileges while also bragging about nuclear arms of savagery and barbarity. **African people currently have nothing in the UN and by walking away from nothing, they will lose just about nothing!**

Conclusion

CKD will not give a number estimate of jobs that will be created out of the Zimbabwe Industrial Evolution or the size of economic growth plus the developed country status for Zimbabwe that will be realised within ten years, for it will not be necessary to count the number of water molecules in a cup of water but what is clear is that Zimbabwe will need expatriate workforce to cope. ZiNdege Corporation and its scope of business among other technologies of the CKD Industrial Evolution have serious business opportunities and potential which will change the image and fortunes Zimbabwe and Africa forever. ZiNdege product line of aircrafts will revolutionise air travel in terms of cost, comfort, equipment aesthetics, equipment aerodynamic performance and safety. Under the leadership of CKD, Zimbabwe will launch at least two space vehicles Mlimo SV 001 for medium distance space explorations followed by Kurumbi CHT2 for super long distance missions into the Galaxies of Kurumbi (Gwara raKurumbi) to retrace the footpath of Kurumbi and put Zimbabwe at super competitive level in technology terms all of which will be signature footprints of the architects of the Great Zimbabwe but now being produced by their descendants which will prompt nations to ask if the legends of Mutota, Nehoreka or Tshaka have come back to life? The Great Zimbabwe was great from the beginning and will forever be great.

The sure way to eradicate poverty in Africa is through the industrialization of Africa in order to get the full value of the abundant natural resources and own the market 100% as envisioned by this CKD Campaign. To prove the futility of world efforts to eradicate poverty, China which has trillions of dollars of business in Africa pledged $2 billion at UN to help eradicate poverty which translates to a few cents per poor citizen in Africa. On that basis any poor nation which is going to follow the foot path recommended by the developed nations to migrate from poverty, will forever remain poor and therefore the onus is on the developing nations to industrialize and own the trillion dollars business owned by China and others in Africa and post back to China their $2 billion dollar donation which actually delays the need to industrialize and causes Africa to lose trillions of dollars for agreeing to accept in the short term, a few cents per poor citizen. If China was a sincere liberation supporter for Africa, then the latter must not feel indebted to China for supporting independence from imperialism by mortgaging the bulk of African resources to China. It will be without logic for Zimbabwe or Africa to expect economic Uhuru or milk and honey from the dog eaters in China when the Chinese are in fact not eating milk and honey but dogs, frogs, snails and snakes, which the poorest in Africa would rather starve to death than eat such cocktails. Africa is too rich for the proprietors thereof to wallow in this abject poverty.

Zimbabwe has a solid technological history and CKD invites the citizens re-trace the foot path of the founding architects, come and ride the technology wave. And after careful analysis of the CKD campaign, if it was in your hands to apportion the sceptre into the rightful hands, would you apportion it to CKD? Citizens are encouraged in this selection process to base their choice on objectivity and not on the basis of being owned by a political party where certain supporters are known to support any unreasonable party decision for reason of master-slave relationship between party and followers even if the political leadership makes daring mistakes. If there happens to be a prospective leader with a better manifesto than the CKD Campaign, this campaign will be rested and CKD will rally all citizens to the best manifesto.

The greatest empowerment that Zimbabweans obtained from Gushungo was education for out that empowerment, Zimbabweans can stand shoulder to shoulder with any nation in all fields of knowledge. The first space vehicle from Africa (Mlimo SV001) will navigate the outer space from Zimbabwe while the first passenger jet from Africa (ZiNdege 102/103) will take off from Zimbabwe from the foundation of that education. Everything is there in Africa except self belief which was killed by imperial subjugation and the CKD brief is to regenerate the self belief of the fore bearers.

If Robert Mugabe who is already chosen is separated from the prospective candidates in Zimbabwe and people wind back to the greatest of Zimbabwe like Sekuru Chaminuka, Mlimo, Nehanda, Kaguvi and Mukwati, if they were to recommend a leader with the grand vision of the Great Zimbabwe, who would they recommend to succeed the incumbent?

Citizens who share the same view of issues laid out in this CKD Campaign — Leadership After Robert Mugabe: The Zimbabwe Industrial Evolution document, are requested to buy a copy or recommend to a friend on Amazon.com, visit Youtube, Facebook or @CKD Campaign on Twitter to steam-roll the campaign.

Index

abortion   57, 58
academics   46, 53
accounting   33
aerodynamic   5, 28, 62
aeroplane   5, 6, 7, 18, 28, 45
aerospace   5, 6, 22, 23, 32, 33
aerospace engineering 23, 32, 33
aerospace vehicle 7, 21, 26, 33
African Culture 13, 14, 48, 55, 56
African Dialects   14
African identity   13
African Industrialization 7, 22, 62
African Language   14
African Traditions   13, 46, 48,
                      56, 60
Africa University   12, 39, 45,
                      50, 58
Airbus   18, 29
air compressors   6
air-conditioning 6, 25, 41, 42, 45
aircraft engineering 23, 29
aircraft ground power   29, 30
airfield lighting 36
airplane   5, 6, 25, 26
air ticketing and reservation 33
alcohol   5, 50, 51
A-Level   14, 15, 16, 30
Alstom   28, 36
Allen Bradley   33
alternator   27
amadlozi   11, 55
amahlayi   14
amazinyo azagegeza   20
Amazon   2, 63
America 5, 6, 7, 8, 17, 18, 19, 21,
    22, 26, 35, 42, 46, 50, 52
American 18, 21, 22, 32, 39, 43,
                      46, 52
American Challenger   6
amplifier   40, 41
Amsterdam   9
angle   37
antennae   33, 41
Anti-Corruption Commission 49
anti-poaching   47
anti-retroviral   50
anti-viral software 25, 33, 45
Apple   19
application system   25, 33, 45
Applied Chemistry   30, 31
Apps   25, 33, 45
Armageddon   22

artist   53
Asia   6, 7, 8, 26, 32, 35, 38,
         40, 49
Asian   14, 26, 39, 43, 47
attenuator   40, 41
attorney   48, 56
audio visual   6, 25, 40, 41, 45
auto mobile   6, 27, 35, 39
African Union Army (AUA) 61
AUA - Egyptian Battalion 61
AUA - Great Zimbabwe Battalion
         61
AUA - Nigerian Battalion 61
Austria   20
author   53
aviation   5, 22, 23, 29
aviation systems   6, 25, 29, 45
Aviation and Aircraft Engineering
                     28, 29
avionics   5
Baggage Handling System 29
Bahlinja   7
Banda Robson, MP   53
banking   33
batteries   14, 27, 30
Baya Raisedon, MP   53
bearing   27, 37
Beira-Mutare-Harare Pipeline 30
Belgium   20
Benhura Dominic, MP   53
Benzi   52
Bernoulli Daniel   28
bicycle   26, 27, 45
Bindura University of Science
Education   28, 33, 45, 61
Bing   33
Biology   10, 15
birth canal   50
Black Byron, MP   53
blast furnace   5
Bloch Eric, MP 53
blood centrifuge   5, 37
blood pressure 5
BMW   6
Boeing   18, 29
Boers   6
Bombardier   28, 29
boom spray   6
Borrowdale   17
Brazil   22
Bridgestone   27, 31

broadcasting equipment 6, 25,
                      41, 45
Brother   43
Bulawayo   17
Bulawayo Polytechnic 12, 28, 30,
    31, 32, 33, 39, 40, 41, 45
Bulawayo University   23
Bulilima   52
bullet train   6
bus   25, 28, 45
buying and selling economy 7
cable   33, 34, 35, 41, 45
cable television 15, 16
Caesarean mutilation   50
calibrated container   5
camera   25, 40, 41, 45
Cambridge   23, 46
Cannon   40
capacitance   37
carbon dioxide 6, 31, 61
CASE   40
Caterpillar   40
Catholic University of Zimbabwe
    33, 34, 35, 45, 60
Caucasian   13, 17
Caucasian hair 13
Caucasus Mountain   5, 17
Centre for Democratic Studies 23
Centre for Peace Dynamics 23
cervical cancer 57
Cessna   29
CFM International   28
Chakaipa Patrick, MP   53
chakata   12
Chaminuka, Sekuru   63
Chavhunduka Gordon, MP 53
chechete   12
Chemical Engineering   30, 31
Chemistry   10, 15, 30
Chenjerai Susan, MP   53
Chetsanga Christopher, MP 53
Chevrolet   27
Chiadzwa   5, 40
Chibadura John, MP   53
Chibero   11, 45, 59
Chibero University   23
Chidyamatovo 15
Chidzero Bernard, MP   53
chief executive officer 6, 55
Chief Justice   51
Chigaduro GR50   6, 40
Chilonga   15, 52

Index

Chikomba, Chief   55
Chikuku   52
chimanda-manda   57
Chimanimani   17
Chimbetu Simon, MP   10, 53
Chimoio   11
Chimurenga War   11
Chimusasa Tendai, MP   53
China   5, 7, 21, 22, 37, 60, 62
Chinese   7, 14, 21, 31, 62
Chingaira, Chief   55
Chinhoyi Battle   46
Chinhoyi University of
Technology   36, 37, 42, 45
Chiredzi   15, 16, 17
Chirinda   52
Chishamiso High School 16
chishava   57
Chitekedza, Chief   55
Chitundumutsere-mutsere   6, 32
Chiweshe Stella, MP   53
cholesterol   59
Christopher Columbus   19
Chrome   33, 37
Chromium   37
Chunga Moses, MP   53
Citroen   27
CKD Slogan   54
clean water   59
closed circuit television 46
clinical manometer   37
cloud base   37
Coalition of Political Scientists 23
coaxial cable   41
cockpit   5
colonial administration 9
combine harvester   6, 38
combustion engine   31
compactor   40
computing   22
concrete mixer   40
construction equipment 6, 25,
                       40, 45
continuous improvement 23
Control and Command Centre
                       23, 33
controller   26
conveyor belt   5, 30
coolant   27
coordinator   55
Corruption 11, 17, 49, 53, 56, 57
cotton   7, 11, 43

crane   40
credit rating agency   20
crime   46, 47, 48, 49, 54, 56, 57
crude oil   30
crusher   35, 40
current   37
curriculum vitae   51, 54
cutting instrument   6, 35, 37, 38
Dabengwa Dumiso, MP   53
dale   9, 52, 54, 56
Dangarembga Tsitsi, MP 53
dare   9, 52, 54, 56
Databases   25, 33, 45, 53, 56
Davos Economic Forum   22
death penalty   47
decoder   41
deed of transfer 56, 59
Dembo Leonard, MP   53
delele   58
derere   58
detainee   10, 11, 53
Distance   37
Docking Guidance System 29
Dog Culture   13, 14, 57
Dog meat   7, 62
Dotito   5, 52
D.R. Congo   19, 20, 50
drilling machine 24, 37, 38, 40
drive belt   24
Dube Fanyana, MP   53
Dunlop   31
Dzivaresekwa   17
earth mover   25, 28, 39, 45
economic break-free   19
economic injustice   21
economic uhuru   20, 62
economist   53
Egypt   5, 17, 44
Egyptians   50
e-learning   16
electricity   20
electric motor   5, 14, 17, 24, 35,
                       42
electromagnetic waves 5, 16, 37
electro-mechanics   22
electronic chip 26, 31
elephant tusk trading tariff 47
elevation   37
elevator   35, 42
Embraer   29
encoder   41
environmental pollution tariff 61

escalator   35, 42
Esigodini   11, 45, 59
Esigodini University   23
ethernet   33
Ethiopia   18
Europe   6, 7, 8, 12, 17,
                18, 19, 20, 21, 22, 26,
                32, 35, 40, 49, 50, 54, 61
Europeans   6, 7, 9, 13, 14,
                18, 19, 20, 21, 22, 24, 26, 28, 32,
                39, 43, 47, 49, 50, 51, 59
European Central Bank 19
European Union   21, 28
Evangelism   10
excavator   25, 28, 45
exhaust   27, 31
Explorer   33
exotic hair styles   13
Ezekiel Guti University 33, 34,
                35, 45, 58, 60
Facebook   2, 33, 63
family planning   50
Far East   17, 21, 22
farm equipment 6, 25, 38, 43, 45
Fascists   62
Federal Reserve Bank   19
feeder cable   34, 41
female liberty   58
fertilizer   20
Feruka Oil Refinery 5, 6, 25, 30,
                31, 45
fibre optics   16, 33, 41
Fire Fox   33
Firestone   31
First Chimurenga War   9, 11
flow   37
FMT   29
food basket   58
Forestry Commission   12, 45
Forestry University   23
Form1:   15
Form6   15, 16
Forward with Me   54
Forward with Zimbabwe 54
fossil fuel   31
France   20, 21, 60
fraud   46
French   14, 21
frequency   37
fruit trees   12, 45
Galaxies of Kurumbi 32, 33, 62
Garden of Eden 12

Index

Gazaland 5, 42
gender abuse 48
gender equality 52
gender infection 48, 56, 57
gender mutilation 50
General Electric 28, 36
general manager 6, 55
Genesis ch2: 18
Germany 18, 20, 42
Gihon 18
ginnery 43
Giza 5, 17, 18, 26, 44
global pollution 31, 39, 61
GMC 27
GMO foods 21, 59
gnashing of teeth 20, 21, 49, 61
Gokwe 5
Goodyear 31
Google 33
grader 6
Grain Marketing Board 12
grain reserve 12
gravity separator 40
Great Zimbabwe University 40, 41, 42, 45
Greece 19, 20, 21, 52, 54
Green Market Sakubva 5, 42
growth hormones 59
Growth Point 17
GSM/mobile/XG 33
gun-less society 46, 52
Guramatunhu Solomon, MP 53
Gushungo 8, 58, 63
Gwabayana, Chief 55
Gwanda State University 38, 39, 40, 45, 58
Gwara raKurumbi 17, 32, 62
Gwebi 11, 45, 59
Gwebi University 23
Gweru 17, 23
Gweru Polytechnic 27, 35, 45
Gweru University 23
hacha 12
haemodialysis machine 37
Harare 17
Harare Institute of Technology 23, 30, 31, 36, 45
Harare Polytechnic 28, 29, 33, 35, 41, 45
Harare University 23
Harvard 23, 46
Havilah 18

hay 12, 59
Head of State 6, 40, 52, 54, 59, 61
health insurance 49
health policy 49
Hebrews 10, 50
hi-fi 41
Highfields 5, 42
high speed train 6, 17, 18, 25, 28, 29, 45
HIV-AIDS 48, 50, 57
Hlomani 16
Holland 7, 20
Hollywood 11
homework 16
Honeywell 29, 36
hosho 14
hot dog 5, 17, 32, 61
Hove Chenjerai, MP 53
hubvu 12
humidity 37
hunger situation 12
hute 12
hwakwa 12
Hyundai 27
Imbwa yangu Machena 7
IMF 20
incubator 38
India 5, 7, 21, 22, 37, 60
Indian 5, 21
inductance 37
industrial instruments 6, 25, 37, 45
industrial process control 5, 22
ingun'u 14, 40
Injiba 6, 26, 27, 54, 55
Instagram 33
instruments 6, 25, 36, 37, 45
intelligent chip 26
International Aero Engines 28
International Law 9
internet navigator 25, 33, 45
intimidation 53
inverter 30
Irrigation system 12, 38, 52, 53, 58
iron and steel refinery 5
isisebenzi sidalansimbi 24
Isitimela Corporation 17, 28
isitshwala 5, 30
Isitshwala ngibulale 49
Israel 60

Italy 20
Jacaranda 12
Jakwara/Nhimbe 12: 6, 38
Japan 18, 26, 42
Japanese 26
Johnson Controls 33
Joint Commander-In-Chief 61
Juki 43
Juliasdale 17
Justice System 10, 52, 55, 56, 58
JVC 40
Kaguvi, Sekuru 9, 10, 11, 56, 63
Kairezi 11
Kamba Walter, MP 53
Kariba 17
Karoi 17
Kawasaki 28
Kazakhstan 30
Khumalo Willard, MP 53
KIA 27
Kikuyu 14
Komatsu 40
Kone 42
Kotwa High School 16
Kubatana Technical College 28, 42, 45
Kubatana University 23
Ku Klux 62
kugedageda kwameno 20
Kunenyati Knowledge, MP 53
Kurumbi 17, 32, 33, 62
Kurumbi Space Vehicle CHT2: 6, 17, 32, 33, 62
Kushinga Phikelela 33, 34, 35, 45
Kushinga Phikelela University 23
Kutama 9
kuzvimbirwa 49
Kwekwe Polytechnic 27, 35, 45
Kwekwe University 23
land under-utilization tariff 12
lathe machine 24
Laws of Thermodynamics 5, 30
level 37
Liberation Struggle 8, 9, 10, 11, 55
Libya 61
Lighting Systems 6, 25, 36, 45
liver cirrhosis 51
livestock fattening 59
Lockheed Martin 29
London 9, 18

Index

lorry 28
lubrication oil 30
lude 58
Lundi 11
Lupane 17
Lupane State University 28, 45, 60
Luxembourg 7, 20
Mabweadziva 52, 59
Macheso Alick, MP 53
Macintosh 33
MaComrade 11
Madzikatire Safiriyo, MP 53
Mafia 49, 62
Magandanga 11
magicians 10
magnifying lens 5, 37
Mahlemhlope 17
Majaivana Lovemore, MP 53
Makhurane Phineas, MP 53
Makokoba 5, 17, 30, 42
managing director 6, 55
Mandigora David, MP 53
Mandinga 14
Mangwende, Chief 55
manna 12
Manufacturing internship 23, 45
Mapfumo Thomas, MP 53
mapfura 12
Mapondera, Chief 9, 55
Maraire Dumisani, MP 53
marijuana 50, 51
marimba 14
maroro 12
Mars 17, 33
masawu 12
Mashayamombe, Chief 9, 55
Mashonganyika, Chief 9, 55
mashuku 12
Massachusetts Institute of Technology 23, 46
master farmer 53
Masuku Lookout, MP 53
masvikiro 11, 55
Masvingo 11, 17
Masvingo Polytechnic 12, 39, 40, 41, 42, 45
Masvingo University 23
matamba 12
Matabeleland 16
Matavire Paul, MP 53
Mathematics 10

Matigimu 16
matohwe 12
Matonjeni 52, 59
mauyu 12
mawonde 12
mazambiringa 12
Mazda 26, 27
mazhanje 12
mbambara 12
Mbare 30
mbila 14
mbira 14
mbuya 58
medical equipment 5, 6, 7, 25, 26, 37, 45
Medical Physics 16
medicament 20
medicine 10, 50, 51
Mediterranean Sea 19
Member of Parliament 53, 54, 55
Mercedes Benz 19, 27
metal engineering 24
Mexico 52
mhizha 38
Mhlanga Cont, MP 53
Mhosva Inoripwa 10, 47, 55, 56
mhotsi 13
Michelin 31
microphone 40, 41
microscope 5, 37
Microsoft 19
Midlands State University 27, 45, 60
Middle Ages 48, 53, 59, 62
midwife 53
military hardware 25, 43
millet 11, 58
Mining University 23
missionary 13
mission school 13, 14
Mitsubishi 19, 27, 42
mixer 35, 40, 41
Mlezi 11, 45, 59
Mlezi University 23
Mlimo 9, 10, 11, 55, 63
Mlimo Space Vehicle 001: 6, 17, 32, 33, 62, 63
mobile phone 25, 34, 45
Moses 18, 50
Mosi-oa-Tunya 17
motion picture 11
motor bike 25, 26, 27, 45

motor vehicles 20, 26
moving walk 35, 42
mowa 58
Moyana Kombo, MP 53
Moyo C. Aaron, MP 53
Mozambique 10
Mpfula Kahina 20: 6, 38
Msasa Technical College 28, 39, 45
Msasa University 23
Muammar Gaddafi 61
Muchawaya Ketai, MP 53
Mucheke 30
Muchigere Mbuya 5, 30
mudare 54
mudzanga weChikonde 51
Mudzi 15, 16
Mugabe Robert 7, 8, 9, 63
Mujuru Ephat, MP 53
Mukwamba Patrick, MP 53
Mukwati 63
multiplexer 25, 33, 45
mukunda 57
Mumbai 7
mumisasa 52
Mungoshi Charles, MP 53
Mungoshi Jesesi, MP 53
Munhumumwe Marshall, MP 53
Mupfure Technical College 12, 28, 29, 43, 45
Mupfure University 23
Musa 11
Musikavanhu 13
Musoni 6, 43
Mutare 17
Mutare Polytechnic 12, 39, 40, 41, 42, 45
Mutare University 23
Mutoko 24
Mutota 62
Mutsvairo Solomon, MP 53
Mutukudzi Oliver, MP 53
Mutizwa Stanford, MP 53
Mvema 6, 17, 25, 28, 45
Mvura Naya-naya 20: 6, 39
mvuto nemhizha 24
Mwene Mutapa Building 9
Mwene Mutapa Empire 8
Mwenezi 16
Mzingwane High School 16
NASA 5
national army 46

Index

national cake   17
national registration   49
national study time table 15, 16
national teacher   15, 16
NATO   61
natural agriculture   58
natural birth   50
natural medicine   49, 50
Nazi Concentration Camp 49
Ndarangarira Gamba   10
Ndebele   14, 15
Ndlovu Adam, MP   53
Ndlovu Madinda, MP   53
Ndlovu Peter, MP   53
Ndunduma Stanley, MP 53
Nehanda Mbuya 9, 10, 11, 55, 63
Nehoreka   62
Neo-Nazists   62
Newton Isaac   28
New York   18, 62
NGO   23, 47
ngoma   14, 40
Ngwarati 6, 26, 27, 50, 54, 55
nhengeni   12
nhunguru   12
nhunzvatunzva 58
nhuta   55
nickel   20
Nissan   27
Njelele   52, 59
n'ombe yemudzimu   10
North Korea   60
NSSA   55
nuclear arms   8, 9, 20, 22, 33,
    44, 60, 61, 62
nuclear war   48
nuclear trade tariff 44, 60, 61
NUST   23, 26, 30, 31, 32, 33, 34
    35, 36, 37, 45, 50, 59
Nyadzonia   11
Nyamandlovu   17
Nyamapanda   17
Nyamaropa   52
Nyanga   17
Nyangani, Mt   52
Nyarara Mwana 24, 31
Nyathi Pathisa, MP   53
nyii   12
nyivhi   58
nylon   30
nzvirun'ombe   12
Oil and Gas   5, 6, 22, 25, 30
    45

Old MacDonald 31
O-Level   13, 14, 16
Omron   33
One Class Model 14, 15, 16
Operating System 25, 33, 45
orbit   33
organic agriculture   58
orthodox church   10
oscillator   5, 30, 37
Osram   36
Otis   42
overeating   49
Pakistan   60
Pamberi Neni   54
Pambili Nami   54
Panasonic   40
Passenger Boarding Bridge 29,
    35
Passport Office 49
pet cash   15
Peugeot   6
Phillips   36
Physics   10, 15, 16, 30
pick-up truck   28
pilgrimage   11
Pison   18
planter   38
platinum   20
PLC   25, 33, 45
Plumtree   17
police   16, 46
police clearance   57
Political parties finance act 53
Porsche   17
Portugal   20
power   30, 37
Power Generation   35, 45
power systems 5, 35
Pratt & Whitney 28
precipitation   37
Presidential Residence 52
pressure   33, 37
prison system   47
processor   26
professional   53, 54
prostitution   46
prototype   6, 27
public sector salaries   55
pump   35, 37
racism   61
racism tariff   61
rack   34, 41

radiator   27
radioactivity   15, 16
rape   48, 50, 56
receiver   25, 33, 41, 45
rectifier   30
refrigeration   6, 25, 41, 42, 45
refrigeration compressor 6
religion   5, 13
religious extremism   13, 62
religious schisms   13
religious tolerance   13
remuneration of the president 52
Renault   27
researcher   53
resistance   37
resonance cavity   41
restitution   10
restrictee   10, 11, 53
Rhino horn trading tariff 47
Rhodes   12
Rhodesian Army   11
Rio Tinto   11, 45, 59
Rio Tinto University   23
Robertson John, MP   53
robotics   35
rocket   5
Rolls Royce   28
Roman Jesuits 9
Rome   9, 18
router   25, 33, 45
Russia(n)   14, 60
rukato   12
sadza   5, 30
Sadzandiuraye 49
Safegate   29
Sahi   6
Samsung   19, 26
Sakubva   30, 42
sanctified bull   10
Savannah   11, 58
Save   11
SCADA   33
sceptre   8, 9
Schindler   42
science   10, 13, 14, 15, 18
screw driver   24, 37, 38
SDH   33
search engine 25, 33, 45
secondary school   11, 13, 15
Second Chimurenga War 9, 11
Security council   62
sedan   28

Index

Seke, Chief 55
semi-conductor 6, 16, 25, 26, 33, 40, 45
sensors 5, 6, 25, 36, 37, 45
sewing machine 43
Shakespeare Literature 10
Shangani 14
Shaya George, MP 53
shenje 12
Shona 14, 15
shuma 12
Sibanda Mercedes, MP 53
Siemens 28
sika 12
Silas 11
silk 43
Singer 43
skin bleaching cosmetics 13
Skinheads 62
Skuza Solomon, MP 53
slave cargo 19
slave labour 22
slave mindset 18
slave trade 6, 22, 48, 52, 61
slut 57
small grain 11, 45, 58
small vehicle 25, 26, 27, 45
smoke 37
Spain 20
spanner 37, 38
speaker 40
spirituality 13, 50, 51
social networks 25, 33, 45
sodomy 9, 14, 48, 58
software 6, 25, 33, 45
solder 37
soldier 46, 53, 61
Solusi University 33, 45, 58, 59, 60
Sonet 33
Sony 19, 40
sorghum 11, 58
sosoti 12
sound mixer 40, 41
South Africa 6, 30, 31
speed 37
standard 6: 14
starter 27
State House 52
stethoscope 37
stockfeed 12, 59
Stockholm 30

sugar cane 11
sugar daddy 57
Suv 28
Sweden 30
switch 25, 33, 45
Tagutapadare 49
Takavada James, MP 53
Tangawarima Felix, MP 53
Tangwena Rekai Chief, MP 53
Tauro Shakeman, MP 53
Tavarwisa Sheba, MP 53
Tax System 45, 60
teacher pupil ratio 7
team leader 6, 55
technical kingpin 6
teleconference 15
temperature 5, 37
Telecommunication 5, 6, 16, 22, 33
television 26, 41
Tembwe 11
test equipment 34, 41
Texas 30
textile 6, 25, 43, 45
textile processing machines 6, 25, 43, 45
theft 46
thermometer 37
Thorn 36
Thorn Hill Airbase 23, 33
thug 57
Thula Mntwanami 24, 31
Thyssen 29
time 37
title deed 9, 21, 56, 59
titration 10, 15
tobacco 11
tools 6, 25, 37, 38, 45
Toyota 6, 19, 27
toys 24, 25, 26, 31, 32, 35
toys and games 6, 31, 32, 45
tractor 6, 38
traditional attire 13
traditional healer 53
traditional leader 11, 53, 54, 55, 56
transformer 35
transmitter 25, 33, 37, 41, 45
trophy hunting 47
tsambatsi 12
Tshaka 62
tsine 58

tsubvu 12
tsvoritsvoto 12
turbo generator 5
tyres 26, 30, 31
Twitter 2, 63
Ubadalo 10, 47, 55, 56
udade 57
UK 20, 60
ukufutelwe 49
ultrasound scanner 5, 37
umbwa 13, 57
umdale 54
Umguza 5
Umlimi X01: 6, 38
Umoya 6
Umvelinqangi 13
Umvukela 11
Uncle Xi Chong Chi 31
Unethical sciences 33
United Africa 8
unja 13, 57
Unkulunkulu 13
unwele olude 13
urban rates 59
USA 30, 60
UZ 23, 28, 29, 35, 36, 38, 45, 50, 58
Uzbekistan 30
vacuum cleaner 5, 35
VanaMukoma 11
Vadyi Vembwa 7
Vanhu/Bantu Dialects 14
Vanhu/Bantu Language 14
ventilator 37
veto power 62
Vhumba 17
vibration 37, 40
video conference 15, 54
visibility 37
voltage 37
vote buying 53, 54
wanna-be 5, 8
war veterans 10, 11, 53
war collaborators 10, 11, 53
water reservoir 58
wave guide 33
weaving 43
weed 50, 51
weevils 12
weight 37
welding machine 37
West 7, 12, 17, 19, 32, 49

Index

Westgate Technical College 28, 36, 45
Westgate University   23
Wezhira Steel Belt   6, 27, 31
Whatsapp   33
Windows   33
wind direction   37
wind speed   37
win-win partnership   7, 22
Women University of Africa 43, 45, 60
World Bank   20
World War 2:   18
Xhosa   14
Xirhami/Chando   6, 41
X-Ray machine 5, 37
yinkomo yamadlozi   10
Yokohama   27, 31
Yoruba   14
yarning   43
Youtube   2, 33, 63
Zaka   5
Zakaria Nicholas, MP   53
Zambezi   11
Zambia   10, 18
ZANU   10
Zhombe   52
Zi-102   6, 28, 63
Zi-103   6, 28, 63
Zimbabwe Constitution 9
Zimbabwe Marketing Corporation 15, 50
Zimbabwe National Army 10
Zimbabwe Open University 41, 45, 60, 61
Zimbabwe School of Mining 39, 40, 45
ZINATHA   50
ZiNdege Corporation 28, 29, 62
Zulu   14
Zionist   62
zvidhororo   12
Zvinavashe Vitalis, MP 53
Zvishavane   17